# LONELY PLANET
# ROAD TRIP

## NEW ENGLAND

Kim Grant

**Road Trip** New England
1st edition – July 2004

**Published by Lonely Planet Publications Pty Ltd**
ABN 36 005 607 983

| | |
|---|---|
| Australia | Head Office, Locked Bag 1, Footscray, Vic 3011 |
| | ☎ 03 8379 8000  fax 03 8379 8111 |
| | 🖳 talk2us@lonelyplanet.com.au |
| USA | 150 Linden St, Oakland, CA 94607 |
| | ☎ 510 893 8555  toll free 800 275 8555 |
| | fax 510 893 8572 |
| | 🖳 info@lonelyplanet.com |
| UK | 72–82 Rosebery Avenue, London EC1R 4RW |
| | ☎ 020 7841 9000  fax 020 7841 9001 |
| | 🖳 go@lonelyplanet.co.uk |
| France | 1 rue du Dahomey, 75011 Paris |
| | ☎ 01 55 25 33 00  fax 01 55 25 33 01 |
| | 🖳 bip@lonelyplanet.fr |
| | 🖳 www.lonelyplanet.fr |

This title was commissioned in Lonely Planet's Oakland
office and produced by: **Commissioning Editor** &
**Project Manager** Kathleen Munnelly
**Series Designer** & **Cover Designer** Candice Jacobus
**Regional Publishing Manager** David Zingarelli

**Freelancers: Cartographer** Bart Wright
**Editor** Wade Fox **Indexer** Ken DellaPenta
**Proofer** Michele Posner

© Lonely Planet Publications Pty Ltd 2004.

ISBN 1 74059 572 6

Printed through Colorcraft Ltd, Hong Kong.
Printed in China

# CONTENTS

# FROM THE PUBLISHER

## AUTHOR

### Kim Grant

Kim Grant (www.kimgrant.com) began driving before the legal age limit, and her passion for driving continues unabated. She once took a year off from Mount Holyoke College to tool around the Lower 48 on 'black roads,' as opposed to 'red roads' (state highways versus interstates on an AAA map). Twenty years later – after driving an orange Chevy Monza (it was the '70s), a green Fiat Spider (a great date magnet), a VW Fox (I could sleep in the back), a malachite green Saab 9000T (very nice) and a white VW camper van (the jury's still out) – she's now more determined to avoid 'red states' than 'red roads.' She writes Lonely Planet's *Boston* and *New England* (predominately blue states), *Miami & The Keys* and *Florida*

(the jury is still out), as well as *Cape Cod, Martha's Vineyard & Nantucket: An Explorer's Guide.*

Kim is grateful to T'ai Chi Chih originator Justin Stone, a master Zen storyteller. When someone asked Justin, 'Where are you going?' he acknowledged that he was simply wandering toward the ashram. The woman responded, 'I know a shortcut.' Despite what we might wish, there are no shortcuts. Work today so you can be free (to drive) tomorrow.

## SEND US YOUR FEEDBACK

We love to hear from travelers – your comments keep us on our toes and help make our books better. Our well-traveled team reads every word on what you loved or loathed about this book. Although we cannot reply individually to postal submissions, we always guarantee that your feedback goes straight to the appropriate authors, in time for the next edition – and the most useful submissions are rewarded with a free book. To send us your updates – and find out about LP events, newsletters and travel news – visit our award-winning website: 💻 **www.lonelyplanet.com.**

Note: We may edit, reproduce and incorporate your comments in Lonely Planet products such as guidebooks, websites and digital products, so let us know if you don't want your comments reproduced or your name acknowledged. For a copy of our privacy policy visit 💻 www.lonelyplanet.com/privacy.

---

## HOW TO USE THIS BOOK

Opening hours for places listed in this book apply during summer, except where otherwise noted. When entry fees are not listed, sites are free (although some may request a small donation). Price gradings (eg $10/7/5) indicate admission for adults/students & seniors/children.

### Text Symbols

| | | | |
|---|---|---|---|
| ☎ | telephone | s | single rooms |
| 💻 | Internet available | d | double rooms |
| ⌚ | opening hours | ste | suites |
| Ⓟ | parking available | dm | dorm beds |
| 🏊 | swimming pool | | |

---

**Lonely Planet books provide independent advice. Lonely Planet does not accept advertising in guidebooks, nor do we accept payment in exchange for listing or endorsing any place or business. Lonely Planet writers do not accept discounts or payments in exchange for positive coverage of any sort.**

# INTRODUCTION

*New England.* These two simple words conjure up seductive images. It's easy to imagine white clapboard churches on village greens, granite mountains for hiking, seashores for dreaming, swift rivers for kayaking and rockbound coasts for seafaring. It's also easy to envision year-round exploration: autumnal apple picking and foliage tours, wintertime snowshoeing and skiing, springtime maple sugaring and museum-going, music festivals and dining outdoors on clam 'chowdah' in the summer.

Consider going against the seasonal grain (and traffic patterns), though. Sure, nothing can trump a sizzling Cape Cod beach, but a gloriously gray winter day can also bring unexpected peace. In Vermont, ski season and fall foliage vie for high season honors, but nothing beats tooling around the Green Mountains when they're in their full, green, summertime glory. If you explore coastal Maine before summertime traffic jams tie it up, you'll encounter lobstermen in LL Bean boots rather than urbanites in Patagonia.

Though New Englanders feel a common regional identity, the six states are quite different in character. Observe your mood then pick your route. Feel urbane or lazy? Massachusetts is the region's cultural powerhouse and boasts the lion's share of vacation resorts. Feel like retreating? Vermont has unspoiled peaks and forests, lakes and towns. Feel a rugged individuality surfacing? New Hampshire is famous for its 'live free or die' policies and for the majesty of the White Mountains. Feel like getting lost in, or finding, the last frontier? Maine has more than 3500 miles of indented coastline, remote island communities and wild(ish) Acadia National Park.

# GETTING THERE

Boston's **Logan International Airport** (BOS; ☎800-235-6426; www.massport.org) is the major gateway to the region and is easily accessible from other major airports. It's serviced by all major airlines in the USA. The low-budget **Jet Blue Airways** (☎800-538-2583; www.jetblue.com) now serves Logan.

Consider flying budget-minded **Southwest Airlines** (☎800-435-9792; www.southwest.com) into **TF Green State Airport** (PVD; ☎401-737-4000; www.pvdairport.com) near Providence, Rhode Island; **Manchester Airport** (MHT; ☎603-624-6556; www.flymanchester.com), in southern New Hampshire; or **Bradley International Airport** (BDL; ☎860-292-2000; www.bradleyairport.com), in central Connecticut, which serves all of Connecticut, the Berkshires in Massachusetts and Vermont. **Burlington Airport** (BTV; ☎802-862-9286; www.burlingtonintlairport.com) is Vermont's major airport – about as far away from any other point in New England as you can get.

All the big rental-car agencies are located at most airports, among them **Alamo** (☎800-327-9633; www.alamo.com), **Avis** (☎800-331-1212; www.avis.com), **Budget** (☎800-527-0700; www.budget.com), **Dollar** (☎800-800-4000; www.dollar.com), **Hertz** (☎800-654-3131;

## Crusin' With Kids

If you have kids in tow, try these family fun spots:

- **Apple Picking at Woodstock Orchards** (p7); Woodstock, CT
- **Cape Cod Rail Trail** (p22); South Dennis, Cape Cod
- **York's Wild Kingdom** (p30); York, Maine
- **Palace Playland** (p32); Old Orchard Beach, Maine
- **Cog Railway** (p47); Mt Washington, New Hampshire
- Hayrides and sleigh rides at **Robb Family Farm** (p49); Brattleboro, Vermont
- **Ben & Jerry's Ice Cream Factory Tours** (p60); Waterbury, Vermont

www.hertz.com), **National** (☎800-227-7368; www.nationalcar.com) and **Thrifty** (☎800-367-2277; www.thrifty.com).

# ITINERARIES

New England's intimate scale allows you to get a world away in just a few hours. In fact, no point in the six states is more than a half day's drive from any other point.

## PLAYING HOOKY: ONE OR TWO DAYS

**Route 169, Connecticut.** Pick apples (or, depending on the season, go to an old-fashioned fair), window-shop in Putnam and hike in Pomfret. Stay overnight simply to dine at the Golden Lamb Buttery and then bike through Pachaug State Forest the next day.

**Route 9, Vermont.** Enjoy Brattleboro counterculture, sample local cheese, cruise through covered bridges and soak in Old Bennington. Stay overnight to be active: paddle the river, bike dirt roads or hike a section of the Long Trail.

## A LONG WEEKEND: TWO TO FOUR DAYS

**Kancamagus Hwy, New Hampshire.** You could easily pack a lunch, hike two remote trails and be home for a late dinner. But then you'd miss Franconia Notch, camping in pristine wilderness and dangling your feet in the Swift River. Whatever you do, do not leave without ascending Mount Washington.

**Route 7, The Berkshires, Massachusetts.** Make reservations to see the Boston Symphony Orchestra or a dance performance. Pontificate about crazy modern art at MassMOCA. Decide if what made Norman Rockwell tick still exists. Splurge at the Old Inn on the Green. Enjoy live music at the Helsinki Tea Company. Seek out Bash Bish Falls and Bartholomew's Cobble. Cleanse your system at Kripalu then fill it at Zinc. Bike around Williamstown.

**Route 6A, Cape Cod, Massachusetts.** Visit the Sandwich Glass Museum before wandering Sandy Neck Beach. Lick an ice cream cone from Hallet's. Sip morning coffee from the Brewster Store on your way to the Cape Cod Rail Trail. Watch the waves break at Chatham Light and the sun set from Rock Harbor. Save the majority of time, though, for the Cape Cod National Seashore and Provincetown.

## THE GREAT ESCAPE: A WEEK

**Route 6A, Cape Cod, Massachusetts.** Follow the itinerary above at a more leisurely pace. In Provincetown, hunker down for some serious people watching, bicycle through the dunes, gallery hop, check out the Pilgrim Monument, watch the sunset at Herring Cove, take a dune tour with Art and watch for whales with the Dolphin Fleet. All along the Outer Cape, walk any number of National Seashore trails and miles of pristine beaches.

**Route 100, Vermont.** Buy something strangely useful from the Vermont Country Store. Downhill ski anywhere, but save your cross-country skiing for Stowe. In the summer, mountain-bike down these same trails. Visit the Crowley Cheese Factory in Healdville. Buy maple syrup from the older guy at Granville Gulf Reservation. Float down the White River in an inner tube. Drive Bragg Hill Road during fall foliage.

**Route 1, Maine.** Stay in Portland for two nights, Camden for one or two nights and the Bar Harbor area for three or four nights. Get off the beaten path in Castine and Blue Hill. Do not leave without hiking or biking Mount Desert's carriage roads or getting out on the water, preferably in schooner.

# HIGHLIGHTS

**Best Mile-Long Drive** – Bush Hill, CT (p9)

**Best Three-Mile Hikes** – along the Kancamagus Hwy, NH (p44)

**Best Fall Foliage Tour** – along Route 100, VT (p53)

**Best Art Museum** – MassMOCA, MA (p20)

**Best People Watching** – late night at Spiritus, Cape Cod (p28)

**Best Whale Watching** – Provincetown, Cape Cod (p28)

**Best Covered Bridges** – off Route 9, VT (p48)

**Best Exposed Lighthouse** – Pemaquid Light, ME (p36)

**Best Summer Theater** – Williamstown Theatre Festival, MA (p19)

**Best Local Cheese Purveyor** – Brattleboro Food Co-op, VT (p49)

# ROUTE 169

## MAP 2; CONNECTICUT       32 MILES; 1-2 DAYS

The subtitle for this road trip might well read: 'There's no there there.' And therein lies its appeal. Perhaps nowhere else in New England will you find such an undeveloped green valley so close to major urban areas. Dubbed the Quiet Corner, this stretch of Connecticut is known – when it's known at all – for farmland, rolling meadows, nature walks, tiny villages with mid-19th century houses, antiques and, most significantly, an air of timelessness. For detailed area information, contact **Northeast Connecticut's Quiet Corner** ( ☎ 860-779-6383; www.ctquietcorner.org).

From Boston, take I-90 (Mass Pike; a toll road) west to I-84 south to exit 2 (MA 131 east) towards Sturbridge. At the Southbridge rotary, take MA 169 south (1¼ hours; 70 miles). See the end of this tour for two possible return routes.

# WOODSTOCK

## Population 7200

Across the Connecticut state line from Massachusetts, fields become demarcated by ancient stone walls, whose building blocks testify to the painstaking work of clearing fields. Honorable barns bear witness to the honest work of raising livestock and harvesting the land. The Maple Crest Farm logo is emblazoned on a roof, an obvious marker if you're touring the area from above. Consider getting up, up and away with **Brighter Skies Balloon Company** ( ☎ 860-963-0600; www.brighterskies.com; off CT 171; adult/child $210/125, prices vary with number in party), which offers sunrise and presunset journeys. Rather keep your feet on the ground? Pick your own blueberries, peaches, apples and pears at the old-fashioned **Woodstock Orchards** ( ☎ 860-928-2225; CT 169; ⏰9am-6pm daily). Don't forget the fresh apple cider.

As for humble, quiet Woodstock village, its main claim to fame is the1845 **Roseland Cottage** ( ☎ 860-928-4074; www.spnea.org; CT 169; adult/senior/child $4.50/3/2; ⏰11am-5pm Wed-Sun Jun– mid-Oct). This Gothic Revival, a treasure, is surrounded by formal gardens (planted with a preponderance of roses, of course). In South Woodstock, antiques and collectible stores give way to the **Woodstock Fair Grounds**. The Labor Day extravaganza is big here.

# SLEEPING & EATING

## TAYLOR'S CORNER B&B

☎860-974-0490, 888-503-9057; www.taylorsbb.com; 880 CT 171 West; d $95-140

Restored to period elegance, this 18th-century colonial beauty has three rooms, one suite, more fireplaces than you can count and lovely gardens.

### INN AT WOODSTOCK HILL
☎860-928-0528; www.woodstockhill.com; 94 Plaine Hill Rd, off CT 169, South Woodstock; d $130-195

The largest area inn, the 21-room Woodstock Hill has unparalleled views and upscale rooms with four-poster beds and lots of chintz.

### BEAU SOLEIL BAKERY
☎860-963-2290; 815 CT 169; dishes $3-6; ⏲7am-6pm Mon-Fri, 8am-5pm Sat-Sun

This tiny shed churns out 'old world' stone-baked breads and organic muffins, as well as soups and sandwiches.

### THE GATHERING BASKET
☎860-963-0306; 292 CT 169, S Woodstock; dishes $3-6; ⏲10am-5pm Tue-Fri, 7am-5pm weekends

Although herbivores and carnivores are treated with near equality here, in terms of sandwich selection, the edge goes to carnivores because of offerings by Nodine's Smokehouse. Everyone loves the caramelized onion and goat cheese tart, though.

# ON THE ROAD

Continue along CT 169, the road dotted with craggy maples and gentleman's farms, to US 44 East. The road drops down into a broad valley leading past an almost industrial farm to one advertising a 'milkin' parlour.' After a mere 3 miles, populous **Putnam** (population 9000) comes as a surprise; finally, we have a bona-fide town center, complete with brick mill buildings and the Quinebaug River falls. Formerly a textile town, Putnam is now the region's undisputed antiques capital. You name it, you can find it here. Follow Main St to Monohansett St and the **Great Atlantic Auction Company**, where oversized architectural antiques spill onto the sidewalk. When you work up an appetite, **The Vine** ( ☎860-928-1660; 85 Main St; lunch $7-14, dinner $10-18; ⏲lunch Mon-Sat, dinner Tue-Sun) will grow on you. The storefront New American eatery specializes in fancy pasta dishes and fish, but it also serves salads. As for sleeping, the two-guestroom **Felshaw Tavern** ( ☎860-928-3467; Five Mile River Rd, off US 44 east; d $85) dates to 1742, excels in elegant comfort and takes its history straight from the Revolutionary War.

# POMFRET

## Population 3800

Backtrack on US 44 and continue on CT 169 south. Rock walls become more formal as the prestigious and imposing **Pomfret School** (1894) comes into view. Stop for some hiking and prime bird-watching at the 650-acre **Connecticut Audubon Bafflin Sanctuary** ( ☎860-928-4041; www.ctaudubon.org; 220 CT 169; free; ⏲dawn to dusk). For a different kind of flight, the **Sharpe Hill Vineyard** (☎860-974-3549; www.sharpehill.com; 108 Wade Rd; ☽11am-5pm Fri-Sun; lunch Sun, dinner Fri & Sat) delivers. After sampling some award-winning wines, dine on grilled meats in an old tavern or on a cheese plate in the outdoor garden. To reach it from CT 169, take CT 97 south and turn left on Kimball Farm Rd. Detour west on US 44 for **Mashamoquet Brook State Park** (☎860-928-6121, 877-668-2267 reservations; US 44 W, Pomfret; sites $11; ☽Mid-Apr–mid-Oct), with 55 open and wooded campsites, almost 1000 acres, a swimming pond and good hiking trails.

## SLEEPING & EATING

### CELEBRATIONS INN
☎860-928-5492; www.celebrationsinn.com; 330 CT 169; d $125-200
This early 20th-century Victorian manse boasts 20 rooms but only five are for guests. They're all inviting and terribly comfortable, as are the gardens, big porch, deck and library.

### WINTERGREEN B&B
☎860-928-5741; www.clarkcottageatwintergreen.com; 354 CT 169; d $65-110
Similar in look and feel to its neighbor (above), Wintergreen has four rooms, two of which share a bath.

### THE HARVEST
☎860-928-0008; 37 US 44, off CT 169; dinner $12-25; ☽dinner Tue-Sun, brunch Sun
This popular bistro serves creative cuisine – from Japanese to French to regional American – that's complemented by an extensive wine list.

### VANILLA BEAN CAFE
☎860-928-1562; jct CT 169 & CT 97; lunch $8-10, dinner $11-20; ☽breakfast & lunch daily, dinner Wed-Sun
Most locals return again and again for daily soup specials like butternut squash bisque or smoked chicken sausage gumbo. Dine inside the barn or on the terrace.

# ON THE ROAD

Back on CT 169 south, even though some former farms have been developed with McMansions, your faith in noncommercialism is rewarded with pick-your-own apples at **Lapsley Orchard**. Agriculture still rules. Crossing in to **Brooklyn** (population 7200) in the late winter and early spring, you'll see maple trees draped with sap buckets. And **Bush Hill Rd** rewards drivers with the single prettiest 1-mile stretch on this whole route. Handsome rock walls, even more handsome maples, spotted cows and cleared fields dare you *not* to stop for a photo. Atop the hill, the extraordinary **Golden Lamb Buttery** (☎860-774-4423; 499 Bush Hill Rd, off CT 169, Brooklyn; lunch about $20, dinner $65 per person; ☽dinner Fri-Sat, lunch Tue-Sat

# DETOUR: DON'T STOP NOW

Fortunately **CT 49** south provides an exceptional alternative for reaching I-95, from where it takes 90 minutes to travel 87 miles to Boston. (In fact, this stretch almost physically outshines CT 169.) From Canterbury take CT 14 east to CT 14A east to CT 49 south. It's all here in a 20-mile stretch: roadside farms, silos, wide open fields straddling the two-laner, ridge top views, purple hillsides majesty (at dusk), stately maples, and 18th-century farmhouses with stories to tell. To stretch your legs within Connecticut's largest park, stop at **Pachaug State Forest** ( ☎ 860-376-4075, 877-668-2267 reservations; Voluntown), which abuts the route and offers great mountain biking, hiking and camping within its 30,000 wooded acres.

mid-Apr-Dec) awaits. Guests assemble at 7pm in an antiques-filled barn, mingle over drinks, head off for a hayride and then settle into an award-winning prix-fixe dinner. It's all quite memorable. In order to eat here, you're going to need to sleep nearby, preferably where abolitionist William Lloyd Garrison was married: the **Friendship Valley Inn** ( ☎ 860-779-9696; www.friendshipvalleyinn.com; 60 CT 169; d $140-170), an 18th-century Georgian, offers five rooms outfitted with fireplaces and antiques.

Brooklyn is home to the oldest agricultural fair in the US, the **Brooklyn Fair**, held at the Windham Country Agricultural Society since 1820. Time your visit for the third weekend in August.

The area is also thick with greenhouses and nurseries. Chief among them, **Logee's Greenhouses** ( ☎ 860-774-8038; www.logees.com; 141 North Street, Danielson) dates to 1893 and boasts more than 2000 kinds of indoor plants. From CT 169, take US 6 east to CT 12 north.

As you head out of town, evergreens give way to hardwoods, which are soon replaced by familiar fields. Rock walls slice up fields like scars, tractors take to the roads, and as you come across the crest at **Canterbury** (population 4700), the most perfectly sited farm in the world exposes itself. Long easterly views are a visual delight. For a dose of far more serious matters, the 1805 **Prudence Crandall House** ( ☎ 860-546-9916; CT 169; adult/senior & child $3/2; 10am-4:30pm Wed-Sun Apr-mid-Dec) honors the woman who, despite huge personal costs, stood her ground as head of the first US academy to accept African American women (in 1833).

Continue south on CT 169 for another 11 miles (much of which is similarly scenic) to I-395, which runs parallel to CT 169 and hooks up with the Mass Pike or CT 2 west to Hartford. Or better yet, take the so-called 'detour,' above.

# ROUTE 7 – THE BERKSHIRES

**MAP 3; MASSACHUSETTS**                    **90 MILES; 2-4 DAYS**

Few places in America combine high culture with rural countryside as well as the Berkshires. With more than 50 major cultural attractions – including the country's largest contemporary arts center (MassMOCA) and the Boston Symphony Orchestra's summer home – the Berkshires draw society mavens from Manhattan and Boston. On summer weekends, when the sidewalks are scorching, city dwellers jump in their cars and head for the cool Berkshire breezes to hike, bike, canoe, swim and scavenge for antiques. Fall foliage lingers here late into October, long after the last leaves have fallen in northern New England. In winter, snowshoeing and cross-country skiing are popular.

From the highest point in the state – Mt Greylock (3491ft) – southward to the Connecticut state line, the Berkshires have been a summer refuge since the rich and famous (from Andrew Carnegie to Edith Wharton) arrived in the early 1900s to build 'summer cottages' of grand proportions. Many of these relics survive today as inns or venues for world-class theater, music and dance. We couldn't begin to illuminate the wealth of cultural offerings here; contact the **Berkshires Visitors Bureau** (☎413-443-9186, 800-237-5747; www.berkshires.org) for more details.

From Boston head 2¼ hours and 134 miles west on I-90 (Mass Pike; a toll road) to Exit 2. To return to Boston from Williamstown, take MA 2 east for 145 miles (3 hours).

# ON THE ROAD

Though there's nothing wrong with **Lee** (population 2020), incorporated in 1777, most people barrel through it, forgetting that they're no longer on the turnpike. Take US 20 west into Lee for a study in the 'old' Berkshires – it's a town where the Main Street Five & Dime is classic and where paper is still manufactured. Lee offers a clear choice of lifestyles at breakfast. **Juice and Java** (☎413-243-3131; 60 Main St; ⏰7am-5pm) builds grilled eggplant sandwiches, while **Joe's Diner** (☎413-243-9756; 63 Center St; ⏰5:30am-9pm Mon-Fri, 5:30am-6:30pm Sat, 7am-2pm Sun) is the epitome of Americana. Norman Rockwell's famous painting of a policeman sitting at a counter talking to a young boy, *The Runaway* (1958), was inspired by this diner.

To reach the 16,500-acre **October Mountain State Forest** (☎413-243-1778, 877-422-6762; www.state.ma.us/dem) take US 20 west to Center St and follow signs. This park boasts the largest tract of green space in Massachusetts and 45 good **campsites** (☎877-422-6762; Center St; sites $10-12) near the shores of the Housatonic River.

Seven miles east of Lee along US 20/MA 8, **Becket** is the site of **Jacob's Pillow Dance Festival** (☎413-243-0745; www.jacobspillow.org; $18 to $55; ⏰mid-Jun-early Sep), one of the premier summer dance festivals in the USA. Through the years, Alvin Ailey, Merce Cunningham, Martha Graham, Bill T Jones, Arnie Zane and other leading interpreters of the dance have taken part.

Backtrack to US 20 east and detour 4 miles to the tiny village of **Tyringham**, where you'll find **Santorella** ( ☎413-243-3260; Main St), the gingerbread fantasy studio of Henry Hudson Kitson. Just south of town, the valley opens up with breathtaking views.

Backtrack again to the junction of US 20 and MA 102 and head south on MA 102. Drive or hike to the summit of Mount Wilcox (2112ft) within **Beartown State Forest** ( ☎413-528-0904, 877-422-6762; www.state.ma.us/dem; sites $5-6). Although RVs have trouble getting up the road, tenters can bed down at 12 simple sites overlooking Benedict Pond.

# STOCKBRIDGE

## Population 2275

Stockbridge, whose central district is only a few blocks long, is a picture-perfect New England village, almost too perfect – the way Norman Rockwell might have seen it. Head west on MA 102 for a few blocks to see the big estates and a handful of historic homes. Summer crowds swell the streets, shops and front-porch rockers of the grand old **Red Lion Inn** ( ☎413-298-5545; www.redlioninn.com; 30 Main St; d $90-435). The very heart of Stockbridge, this huge 108-room white-frame hotel is also Stockbridge's premier place for dining. Forgo the elegant formal dining room (mains $21-30) for the rustic colonial pub (mains $9-19). Or head to **Once Upon a Table** ( ☎413-298-3870; 36 Main St; dinner $16-24; ⏱lunch, dinner 5-9pm Thu-Tue), which serves upscale fare, like pan-seared sea bass or sweet potato–filled ravioli, on its glass-enclosed porch. The **Stockbridge Lodging Association** ( ☎413-298-5200; www.stockbridg echamber.org; 6 Elm St) is a useful resource.

## SIGHTS & ENTERTAINMENT

### NORMAN ROCKWELL MUSEUM

☎413-298-4100; www.nrm.org; MA 183; adult/child $12/free; ⏱10am-4pm

The museum has the largest collection of Rockwell's original art and contains his studio (moved here from behind his Stockbridge home). Take MA 102 west to MA 183 south.

### CHESTERWOOD

☎413-298-3579; www.chesterwood.org; 4 Williamsville Rd; family/adult/youth $25/10/5; ⏱10am-5pm May-Oct

Daniel Chester French (1850–1931) created *The Minute Man* (1875) statue at the Old North Bridge in Concord and the great seated statue of Abraham Lincoln in the Lincoln Memorial in Washington, DC (1922). Visit the sculptor's house and barnlike studio filled with nearly 500 pieces of sculpture, finished and unfinished. Take MA 102 west, turn left onto Glendale Middle Rd, and left onto Williamsville Rd.

## BERKSHIRE BOTANICAL GARDEN
☎413-298-3926; www.berkshirebotanical.org; MA 102; adult/senior/child $7/5/ free; ⏰10am-5pm

This 15-acre garden, within walking distance of the Rockwell Museum, is lush with wildflowers, herbs, perennials, water plants, an alpine forest and rock gardens.

## NAUMKEAG
☎413-298-3239; www.thetrustees.org; 5 Prospect St; tours adult/child $10/3; ⏰10am-5pm late May–mid-Oct

This grand Berkshire 'cottage' was designed in 1885 by Stanford White for diplomat and noted art collector Joseph Hodges Choate. His summer house is filled with Oriental carpets, Chinese porcelain and other luxury goods; the gardens are stunning. From the Red Lion Inn take Pine St to Prospect St.

## BERKSHIRE THEATRE FESTIVAL
☎413-298-5576; www.berkshiretheatre.org; tickets $18-31; ⏰late Jun–early Sep

These folks stage new and innovative plays at the Main Stage and smaller Unicorn Theatre.

# ON THE ROAD

Head south on US 7, and vistas start opening up and the lazy Housatonic River begins ambling back and forth across the road. Consider taking one of two summit trails up **Monument Mountain** (1700ft). Writer Nathaniel Hawthorne wrote that Monument's summit resembled 'a headless sphinx wrapped in a Persian shawl.' On August 5, 1850, Hawthorne climbed up Monument Mountain with Oliver Wendell Holmes and Herman Melville. It was the first time Hawthorne and the young Melville met, but they quickly became good friends and kept in touch throughout their lives.

## Norman Rockwell

The illustrator Norman Rockwell (1894–1978) was born in New York City, and he sold his first magazine cover illustration to the *Saturday Evening Post* in 1916. In the following half century, he did another 321 covers for the Post, as well as illustrations for books, posters and many other magazines. His clever, masterful, insightful art made him the best-known and most popular illustrator in US history. His wonderful sense of humor can be seen in his painting *Triple Self Portrait* (1960), in which an older Rockwell looks in a mirror, only to paint a much younger version of himself.

# GREAT BARRINGTON

## Population 2460

Great Barrington's formerly old-fashioned Main St has given way to artsy boutiques, groovy coffeehouses and trendy storefront eateries. While Barringtonians are still down-to-earth, they are beginning to refer to their town as 'Little SoHo,' appealing to city travelers who flood Great Barrington's streets on summer and fall weekends. Little Railroad Street is rife with funky shops and eateries. For more information, contact the **Southern Berkshire Chamber of Commerce** ( ☎413-528-1510, 800-269-6062; www.greatbarrington.org; 362 Main St).

## SLEEPING, EATING & ENTERTAINMENT

### BRIARCLIFF INN
☎413-528-3000; 506 Stockbridge Rd; d in-season/off-season from $175/$55
Across from Monument Mountain on a more scenic stretch of US 7 than in-town motels, Briarcliff's rooms have been renovated and offer air conditioning, TV and king-size beds.

### MANOR LANE B&B
☎413-528-3458; 145 Hurlburt Rd; d from $125; ☺Jun-Oct
Nestled between horse farms, and a five-minute drive from town, this large house has three spacious rooms, a cozy sitting room with piano and Turkish carpets, a glassed-in breakfast area, a pool, tennis courts and adjacent trails.

### THE OLD INN ON THE GREEN
☎413-229-3131, 800-286-3139; www.oldinn.com; MA 57, New Marlborough; d $195-365
Ten miles east of town along lovely back roads, the Old Inn (circa 1760) is exactly what most people picture when they think of a New England country inn. The inn offers five guest rooms with fireplaces and an excellent restaurant lit entirely by candlelight. Windsor chairs and mahogany tavern tables furnish the dining rooms. In the summer, dinner is served outside on the garden terrace. Rooms have 18th-century furnishings and decor, with private baths.

### BABA LOUIE'S
☎413-528-8100; 284 Main St; dishes $4-16; ☺11:30am-9:30pm
Baba's is known for wood-fired pizza with organic sourdough crust.

### HELSINKI TEA COMPANY
☎413-528-3394; 284 Main St; mains $7-20; ☺11am-9:30pm Thu-Tue
Head to the back of the small arcade, plop down on an overstuffed sofa and order a pot of green tea. The eclectic menu features Moroccan-style lamb and the Sibelius barbecue, a honey-orange roasted half chicken named for Finland's most famous composer. On weekends, the coffeehouse-bar features musical acts like Pete Seeger and the

John Scofield Project. The crowd is hip, ranging from carpenters and waitresses to Mia Farrow and James Taylor. Covers run $5 to $35.

## UNION BAR & GRILL
☎413-528-6228; 293 Main St; dishes $12-20; ☺5-10pm Wed-Mon, noon-3pm weekends

One of the Berkshires' hottest restaurants, complete with metallic walls, this moderately priced restaurant offers intriguing dishes like portobello lasagna and duck quesadillas served on aluminum tables.

## CASTLE ST CAFÉ
☎413-528-5244; 10 Castle St; mains average $17; ☺5-10pm Wed-Mon

Chef/owner Michael Ballon uses lots of local ingredients like Hillsdale chèvre cheese and Pittsfield fettuccine to create innovative dishes. Not hungry? Hang out at the cool piano bar, whose piano once belonged to Nat King Cole, who owned a summer home in Tyringham.

## THE BERKSHIRE OPERA COMPANY
☎413-644-9998; www.berkshireopera.org; tickets $45-85

These folks stage full-dress productions of classic and modern operas in the restored Mahaiwe Theatre and at other nearby venues.

# ON THE ROAD

Continue south past picturesque graveyards, old-fashioned fairgrounds, egalitarian antique shops and increasingly rarified ones on US 7 as you head into **Sheffield** (population 3350), on the National Register of Historic Places. Stop at the **Sheffield Covered Bridge** before arriving in Sheffield proper. Although Sheffield is lined with gracious B&Bs, consider staying at the 21-room **Race Brook Lodge** ( ☎413-229-2916; www.rblodge.com; MA 41; d in-season/off-season $120-275/$95-145), a 200-year-old converted barn situated at the base of Mt Race. Take the strenuous trail behind the lodge to Race's summit and a nice ridge walk.

Head south on MA 7A to **Bartholomew's Cobble** ( ☎413-229-8600; adult/child $4/1; ☺9am-5pm mid-Apr–mid-Oct), a high, rocky knoll of limestone, marble and quartzite. These knobby, curious hills are encompassed in a 277-acre reserve cloaked in trees, ferns, flowers and moss. There are 6 miles of hiking trails, including the Ledges Trail, which weaves along the Housatonic River.

Backtrack to Sheffield and turn left at the stocky white church toward MA 41, where you'll head north past hilltop farms dating to the 1700s. Follow signs for Mt Washington State Forest and **Bash Bish Falls**, a scenic waterfall that plunges down a 1000ft gorge.

To really experience back-roads Berkshires, stay overnight at **Baldwin Hill Farm B&B** ( ☎413-528-4092; www.baldwinhillfarm.com; 121 Baldwin Hill Rd, South Egremont; d from $89), off MA 71. It has four rooms, a pool and more than 400 acres of hilltop land with glorious views of the surrounding mountains. The area around here is the stuff of the southern Berkshires: rolling hills, farmlands, quiet back roads.

Head back through Great Barrington on MA 41 to **West Stockbridge** (population 1400). Though not nearly as picturesque as Stockbridge, handsome but blue collar West Stockbridge still retains its historic charm. Old country stores and the 19th-century train station stand next to sophisticated galleries and studios. To quench your cravings, **Caffe Pomodoro** ( ☎413-232-4616; 6 Depot St; dishes $4-10; ☻breakfast & lunch year-round, dinner Thu-Sun in summer), housed in the 1838 railroad station, offers large sandwiches and freshly made soups (try the tomato and fennel). For a worthy splurge, **The Williamsville Inn** ( ☎413-274-6118; www.williamsvilleinn.com; MA 41; r from $155; dinner mains $17-23), a 1797 farmhouse with 16 rooms, creaks with history. Thick wood floors, exposed beams and red-brick fireplaces are de rigueur. The inn is ideal for an intimate candlelit dinner of butterfly pasta served with roasted red peppers, garden peas, garlic and pine nuts.

From the center of town, bear right on Lenox Rd for a nice 4-mile back road to Lenox. You'll come to a screeching halt at **Yokun Ridge Forest Reservation**, which boasts a stunning viewpoint. Depending on the season, the area is popular with hikers and snowshoers.

# LENOX

## Population 1670

This gracious town is a historical anomaly. Its charm was not destroyed by the Industrial Revolution, and then, prized for its bucolic peace, the town became a summer retreat for wealthy families who had made their fortunes by building factories in other towns. Lenox is home to Tanglewood, an incredibly popular summertime music festival, as well as **Shakespeare & Company** ( ☎413-637-3353; www.shakespeare.org; tickets $12.50-35; ☻Tue-Sun), which performs the Bard's great plays. Contact the **Lenox Chamber of Commerce** ( ☎413-637-3646; www .lenox.org; Walker St) for more detailed information. Lenox, by the way, has more white picket fences than you'd ever care to paint. As you head north on US 7 out of town, stop at the quintessential hilltop church, framed by an old graveyard.

## SIGHTS & ACTIVITIES

### THE MOUNT
☎413-637-1899; www.edithwharton.org; 2 Plunkett St at US 7; tours adult/ student/child $16/8/free; ☻9am-5pm May-Oct
Almost 50 years after Nathaniel Hawthorne left Lenox, Edith Wharton came (in 1899) to build this palatial estate. She summered here for a decade, and when not writing, entertained friends like Henry James.

### PLEASANT VALLEY SANCTUARY
☎413-637-0320; 472 W Mountain Rd; $4; ☻sunrise-sunset
This 1112-acre wildlife sanctuary has several pleasant walking trails through forests of maples, oaks, beeches and birches. From US 7 turn left onto W Dugway Rd and continue for 1½ miles.

## BIKING & SKIING

Kennedy Park in downtown Lenox is popular with mountain bikers and cross-country skiers. The **Arcadian** (☎413-637-3010; US 7) rents bikes, cross-country skis, snowshoes, tents and sleeping bags.

# SLEEPING & EATING

Because of Tanglewood, many inns require minimum stays on summer weekends. That means a Lenox weekend can cost $280 to $500 just for lodging.

### WALKER HOUSE

☎413-637-1271; www.walkerhouse.com; 74 Walker St; d $90-220

This conveniently located, modest-looking inn has the friendliest innkeepers in town. Eight guest rooms are surrounded by 3 acres of gardens.

### THE VILLAGE INN

☎413-637-0020; www.villageinn-lenox.com; 16 Church St; d $85-225

This Federal-style inn was built in 1771 and has 32 rooms. The traditional dining room serves breakfast, afternoon tea and dinner, and the tavern concentrates on English ales, draft beer and light meals.

### BLANTYRE

☎413-637-3556; www.blantyre.com; Blantyre Rd; d from $375; ☉May-Nov

If money is no object, then this is the place. An imitation Scottish Tudor mansion built in 1902, the 23-room Blantyre sits on 85 acres of grounds dotted with four tennis courts, croquet lawns, a swimming pool, hot tub and sauna.

### KRIPALU

☎413-448-3400; www.kripalu.org; MA 183; dorm beds from $92, including meals and workshops

One of America's finest yoga centers is set on 300 spectacular acres and can accommodate some 300 students, who come to study yoga and meditation in peaceful surroundings.

## Music in the Hills

Since its start in 1934, the **Tanglewood Music Festival** (☎413-637-1600, 617-266-1492, 800-347-0808; www.bso.org; 297 West St; tickets $18-93; ☉late Jun–early Sep) has been among the most esteemed music events in the world. The performance lineup ranges from symphonies and chamber music to pop, jazz and blues. Most attendees arrive three or four hours before concert time, stake out a listening spot on the lawn, then enjoy elaborate picnics. Lawn space is often still available two or three hours before concerts.

### CAROL'S RESTAURANT
☎413-637-8948; 8 Franklin St; dishes $4-8; 6:30am-2pm

You've gotta love the cinderblock walls, fluorescent lights and Carol's effusive personality. Actress Julia Roberts does; she's a breakfast patron here when she's in town. We like to create our own omelets.

### CHURCH STREET CAFE
☎413-637-2745; 69 Church St; lunch under $10, dinner $18-26; Tue-Sat

This mainstay has made customers happy for years with reasonably priced lunches and inventive dinners (Maine crabcakes are always good) served either in a festive dining room or on the deck.

### SPIGALINA
☎413-637-4455; 80 Main St; mains $15-23; 5-9pm Apr-Dec

Worthy of raves, Spigalina serves tantalizing pasta, fish and meat dishes in a Mediterranean ambiance. Don't miss the *zuppa di pesce*, a soup with five kinds of crustacean and calamari.

### ZINC
☎413-637-8800; 56 Church St; dinner $17-21; 11:30am-3pm & 5:30-10pm

Very, very hip. The postmodern decor here is all metal surfaces, light woods and gleaming curves, with doors made of French wine crates. The cuisine features tempting New American offerings like pan-seared halibut with olive tapenade.

### HERITAGE TAVERN
☎413-637-0884; Housatonic St; dishes $4-8; 11am-10pm

If you're looking for the saloon, complete with Guinness on tap and a pool table, this is it. The Heritage has a natural shagginess about it, right down to the chicken wings and jalapeño poppers.

# ON THE ROAD

Although **Pittsfield** (population 46,800) is the service city of the Berkshires, take a minute to stop at **Arrowhead** (☎413-442-1793; www.mobydick.org; 780 Holmes Rd, off US 7; adult/senior/child

---

## DETOUR: HANCOCK SHAKER VILLAGE

The Shakers were among the millennial Christian sects that flourished in the fertile climate of religious freedom in the New World. And **Hancock Shaker Village** (☎413-443-0188; www.hancockshakervillage.org; US 20; family/adult/child $33/12.50/5.50; 10am-4pm May-Oct), 5 miles west of Pittsfield, will give you a glimpse into their peaceful, prayerful way of life. Occupied by Shakers until 1960, twenty original buildings are carefully restored and are open to view. At its peak, in 1830, the community numbered some 300 souls.

---

$8/5/3; 10am-4pm late May–mid-Oct), where Herman Melville (1819–91) wrote his masterwork *Moby Dick*. Inspired by winter views of whale-shaped Mt Greylock, Melville completed the 600-plus pages in less than a year.

Between stops for maple syrup and farm-stand produce on US 7, you might linger at the long **Pontoosuc Lake**, with the Taconic Mountains of New York state serving as a dramatic backdrop. In winter, downhill skiers will shush down **Jiminy Peak** ( 413-738-5500; www.jiminypeak.com; off MA 43, Hancock), while cross-country skiers will slide over to adjacent **Brodie Mountain** ( 413-443-4752; www.brodiemountain.com; US 7, New Ashford).

Five miles south of Williamstown you'll start swooning over the magnificent views: fields crisscrossed by rock walls, dotted by farmhouses, a church spire here, plenty of grazing cows there.

# WILLIAMSTOWN

## Population 4750

Dominated by prestigious **Williams College**, this academic enclave is full of marble-faced halls, fresh-faced students, outstanding art and exciting summer theater. The **Williamstown Chamber of Commerce** ( 413-458-9077; www.williamstownchamber.com; jct MA 2 and US 7) operates a seasonal booth.

Williamstown and environs, with rolling farmland and quiet country roads, are excellent for biking. Try pretty MA 43, which parallels the Green River. **Mountain Goats** ( 413-458-8445; 130 Water St; bikes $20) rents cycles. It also offers hiking, camping and fly-fishing gear.

A gem among US art museums, **Clark Art Institute** ( 413-458-9545; www.clarkart.edu; 225 South St; adult/children $10/ free; h10am-5pm Tue-Sun) is strong in French Impressionists and the mid-century Barbizon artists. Don't miss Degas' famous *Little Dancer of Fourteen Years*.

One of America's most renowned stages for summer stock, the **Williamstown Theatre Festival** ( 413-597-3399, tickets 597-3400; www.wtfestival.org; late Jun-late Aug) mounts exceptional offerings. Kevin Kline, Richard Dreyfuss and Gwyneth Paltrow are but a few of the actors who have performed here.

## SLEEPING & EATING

### WILLIAMS INN
413-458-9371; www.williamsinn.com; 1090 Main St; d $145-165
On the green, Williamstown's major hotel has a restaurant, indoor pool and 100 luxury-style rooms.

### STEEP ACRES
413-458-3774; 520 White Oaks Rd; d $70-160
Two miles north of town, this 30-acre hilltop farm affords spectacular mountain views, and the furnishings reflect a simple country elegance.

### RIVER BEND FARM

☎413-458-3121; 643 Simmons Rd, off US 7; d from $90; ☾May-Oct

A favorite among European travelers, these four doubles share two baths. A Georgian tavern since revolutionary times, River Bend has been carefully and authentically restored.

### THE GUEST HOUSE AT FIELD FARM

☎413-458-3135; www.thetrustees.org; 554 Sloan Rd; d from $145

Built in 1948 in a spare, clean, post-WWII style and operated by the Trustees of Reservations, this mod five-room house is set on 296 wooded acres. It has a pond, walking trails, a tennis court and a swimming pool. Head south on US 7 to MA 43 west.

### PAPA CHARLIE'S DELI

☎413-458-5969; 28 Spring St; dishes $4-5; ☾8am-8pm

This sunny, welcoming breakfast spot has omelets as well as sandwiches named after the stars who've performed in Williamstown. Richard Chamberlain is stuffed with turkey, Swiss and cranberry.

### HOBSON'S CHOICE

☎413-458-9101; 159 Water St; mains $12-18; ☾5-9pm

Popular with Williams students and faculty, Hobson's has a country-home feel. Lunchtime soups and sandwiches are served in cozy booths. Dinner mains tend toward grilled chicken and seafood pasta.

### MEZZE BISTRO & BAR

☎413-458-0123; 84 Water St; mains $17-25; ☾5-9pm

Actors from the Williamstown Theatre tend to migrate here after performances. Overlooking a waterfall on the Green River, Mezze offers tempting dishes like shiitake mushroom ravioli with celeriac, fennel broth and truffle oil.

# ON THE ROAD

No road trip would be complete without exploring **Mt Greylock State Reservation** ( ☎413-499-4262, 877-422-6762; www.state.ma.us/dem; camping $5-6), Massachusetts's highest peak at 3491ft. Six miles east along MA 2, Mt Greylock has 45 miles of trails and 35 campsites. The ones near scenic Stoney Ledge should be your first choice. Or stay in **Bascom Lodge** ( ☎413-743-1591; Summit Rd; bunks $36, private rooms $98; ☾mid-May–mid-Oct), a fine mountain hostelry built in the 1930s with 32 beds; reservations are essential.

Without a doubt, continue east along MA 2 for another few miles to **North Adams** (population 14,700). The outstanding **Massachusetts Museum of Contemporary Art** (MASS MoCA; ☎413-662-2111; www.massmoca.org; 87 Marshall St; adult/students & seniors/child $9/7/3; ☾11am-5pm) is no ordinary gallery. In fact, it's the largest gallery in the United States. The spaces are large enough to exhibit Robert Rauschenberg's immense *The 1/4 Mile or 2 Furlong Piece*. Grab a bite in the museum cafe.

# ROUTE 6A – CAPE COD

**MAP 4 ; MASSACHUSETTS**                    **120 MILES; 2-4 DAYS**

Miles of unbroken sandy stretches, sturdy lighthouses, roadside clam shacks and blow-up beach toys: this is the stuff of 'the Cape,' New England's favorite summer destination. Pleasure seekers from all over the country come looking for – and find – plenty of fresh seafood, pristine beaches and graceful villages that date back 250 years.

Although this fragile peninsula juts eastward into the Atlantic Ocean for only 65 miles, it has more than 400 miles of shoreline. Even though things get crowded in July and August, come any other time to find a spot to yourself. Only then will the Cape's dune-studded landscapes, tethered by fine stands of tall sea grass and cloaked in scrub oak and pine, hook you.

You'll be in a long line of good company. Mariner Bartholomew Gosnold (1572–1607) sailed this coast in 1602. And when the Pilgrims first set foot in the New World in November 1620, it was at Provincetown, where they drew up the Mayflower Compact, the precursor to the US Constitution. In the mid-19th century, Henry David Thoreau made a walking tour of the Cape and wrote *Cape Cod*.

From Boston, take I-93 south to MA 3 south to the Sagamore Bridge. On an easy traffic day, it takes 1¼ hours to reach the bridge. Then take the rural and scenic MA 6A to Orleans where it becomes US 6 to Provincetown.

# SANDWICH

## Population 21,000

When you cross over the Cape Cod Canal, built from 1909 to 1914 to save mariners the treacherous and time-consuming voyage around the Cape, you will start to feel 'a place apart.' The canal effectively separates Cape Cod from the mainland and makes it an island.

The Cape's first town is also the oldest town and couldn't be more sylvan, centered around a duck pond, the **Dexter Grist Mill** and the circa-1675 **Hoxie House**. If you do nothing else, stop at **Sandwich Glass Museum** ( ☎508-888-0251; www.sandwichglassmuseum.org; 129 Main St; adult/child $4.50/1; ☯ 9:30am-5pm Apr-Dec, shorter hours Feb-Mar), celebrating Sandwich's famous glassmaking heyday from 1825 to 1888.

The nicely landscaped **Shadynook Inn & Motel** ( ☎508-888-0409, 800-338-5208; www.shadynookinn.com; 14 MA 6A; d $95-125 summer, from $65 winter) has 30 clean, simple and large rooms, some of which are efficiencies. Smack in the center of town, **Captain Ezra Nye House** ( ☎508-888-6142; www.captainezranyehouse.com; 152 Main St; d $155/$125 summer/winter), a six-room B&B dating to 1829, has friendly hosts.

For a taste of *Old* England, drop by the ever crowded **Dunbar Tea Room** ( ☎508-833-2485; 1 Water St; dishes $7-14; ☯11am-4:30pm) which specializes in ploughman's lunch, quiche, Scottish shortbread and authentic English tea in a slightly countrified setting. The **Bee-Hive Tavern** ( ☎508-833-1184; 406 MA 6A; lunch $6-10, dinner $8-17) tavern is popular with locals who come for value-conscious servings of pasta, fried seafood, burgers and sandwiches.

# ON THE ROAD

The nowhere-else-but-here ride begins. Businesses start referencing whales; stone walls outnumber neon signs; low-profile cottages and weathered bookshops no longer look out of place. The scale of the world shrinks, even as open vistas draw your attention outward. This winding stretch through **Barnstable** (population 47,800) affords fine glimpses of the ocean and salt marshes. A canopy of trees creates an umbrella over the tight road, shading antique stores, galleries, craft shops and pricey B&Bs. Thus begins the authentic, Cape Cod of (supposedly) yesteryear. On the Sandwich–Barnstable town line, **Sandy Neck Beach** ( ☎508-362-8300; Sandy Neck Rd; P$10) is the bay's best, 6 miles long and backed by an extensive network of dunes. Don't miss it.

Many former sea captains' houses have been converted into romantic B&Bs. The friendly **Honeysuckle Hill** ( ☎508-362-8418, 866-444-5522; www.honeysucklehill.com; 591 MA 6A; d $139-219/$100-180 summer/winter) has four modestly elegant rooms featuring feather beds and white wicker. As for eats, **Mill Way Fish and Lobster Market** ( ☎508-362-2760; Barnstable Harbor; dishes $6-15; ⊗ Mar-Dec) makes great fish sandwiches, fried seafood and fish chowder for takeout. The **Dolphin** ( ☎508-362-6610; 3250 MA 6A; lunch $6-11, dinner $17-22; ⊗ no lunch on Sun), a low-key restaurant and bar and popular local hangout, has a really extensive seafood menu.

Quiet and dignified **Yarmouth** (population 24,800) has even more antique shops and former sea captains' homes. It's the kind of place where white candlesticks flicker in colonial windows, lighting the path from past to present. Stop at the **Captain Bangs Hallet House** ( ☎508-362-3021; 11 Strawberry Lane; adult/child $3/.50; tours 1-3pm Thu-Sun Jun–mid-Oct), once home to a prosperous sea captain who made

## TOURING BY BIKE

The 26-mile paved **Cape Cod Rail Trail** follows an abandoned railroad bed from Dennis to Wellfleet. Along the way you'll pass ponds, forests, a country store or two, a few ocean vistas, beaches and salt marshes. Although some stretches are a tad dull, it's still one of the Cape's most pleasant excursions. Park at the trailhead on MA 134 in South Dennis. Rent bikes ($12/22-27 2hrs/day) and inline skates ($15) at **Barbara's Bike and Sports Equipment** ( ☎508-760-4723; 430 MA 134).

his fortune sailing to China and India. An apothecary in 1889, **Hallet's** (☎508-362-3362; 139 MA 6A; ☼ Apr-Dec), quintessentially 'olde' Cape Cod, still boasts an original soda fountain. Great at sunset, **Grey's Beach**, off Centre St, has a long boardwalk that stretches out into the tidal marsh and across a creek.

Bed down at the old-fashioned **Village Inn** (☎508-362-3182; www.thevillageinncapecod.com; 92 MA 6A; d $70-125; ☼ May-Oct), a family-run hostelry with 10 modest guest rooms of varying sizes. For a sophisticated surprise, **Inaho** (☎508-362-5522; 157 MA 6A; mains $12-23; ☼dinner Tue-Sun) prepares excellent sushi, traditional bento boxes and tempura.

**Dennis** (population 15,000) is studded with cranberry bogs, salt marshes and artisans. Like the rest of MA 6A, it too has its share of little post offices and nonchain gas stations. Dennis serves as a good mid-Cape location for exploring in either direction. The modern and airy **Cape Museum of Fine Arts** (☎508-385-4477; www.cmfa.org; MA 6A; adult/child $7/free; ☼ 10am-5pm Tue-Sat, 1-5pm Sun, winter hours slightly reduced) represents Cape artists working in a variety of media. Climb to the top of **Scargo Tower** (take Old Bass River Rd to Scargo Hill Rd) for views of Provincetown on a clear day. Or wade on in at **Chapin Memorial Beach** (Ⓟ$10), a long, dune-backed beach with a gently sloping grade. The **Cape Playhouse** (☎508-385-3838; www.capeplayhouse.com; 820 MA 6A; tickets $20-38) is generally regarded as the Cape's best summer theater. There's no better venue for foreign, art and independent films than the **Cape Cinema** (☎508-385-2503; www.capecinema.com; 820 MA 6A; ☼ Apr-Nov).

The **Isaiah Hall B&B Inn** (☎508-385-9928, 800-736-0160; www.isaiahhallinn.com; 152 Whig St; d $105-194; ☼ May–mid-Oct), a 19th-century farmhouse, has 11 unpretentious rooms. When hunger strikes, **Gina's By The Sea** (☎508-385-3213; 143 Taunton St; dinner $9-22) is deservedly popular, popular, popular. The traditional northern Italian menu features wickedly garlicky dishes.

# BREWSTER

## Population 8700

Tranquil Brewster is home to the fabled **Brewster Store** (☎508-896-3744; cnr MA 6A & MA 124), an old-fashioned country store in operation since 1866. Pop into the **Cape Cod Museum of Natural History** (☎508-896-3867;www.ccmnh.org; 869 MA 6A; adult/child $7/3.50;☼ 10am-4pm Jun-Sep; call for winter hours) before heading out to nature trails that cross cranberry bogs, salt marshes and beech groves. With 2000 acres, **Nickerson State Park** (☎508-896-3491, 877-422-6762 for reservations; www.state.ma.us/dem/; 3488 MA 6A; camping $15, yurts $25-35; ☼ closed for camping Nov–mid-Apr) boasts 418 wooded sites, eight ponds, lots of bicycling and walking trails, picnic sites and sandy beaches. It's the state's most popular camping place, so reserve early. You'll

## DETOUR: PATRICIAN CHATHAM

This town has a genteel reserve that is evident along its shady Main St. With more than 60 miles of shoreline, it's surrounded on three sides by bays, coves and inlets. From US 6/ MA 6A, take MA 28 south past the very pleasant **Pleasant Bay** to Shore Rd, past the **Fish Pier** to **Chatham Light**. Directly below the lighthouse, dramatic **Chatham Light Beach** is a long, wide sandy beach.

wish you never used the word 'picturesque' before once you see the tranquil and lush **Stony Brook Grist Mill** (830 Stony Brook Rd) and **Herring Run**, adjacent to each other off MA 6A.

The **Old Sea Pines Inn** ( ☎508-896-6114; www.oldseapinesinn.com; 2553 MA 6A; d $75-160; ☾mid-Mar–mid-Dec), a former girls' school, is outfitted with antique iron and brass beds. Some of the 24 rooms have shared bath or a fireplace; others in the rear annex are more motel-like but quite pleasant.

Just off the Cape Cod Rail Trail, **Cobie's** ( ☎508-896-7021; 3260 MA 6A; dishes $3-12; ☾late May-Sep) dishes out requisite fried seafood platters; crunch and munch them at outdoor picnic tables.

Highly regarded for its simple but creatively prepared seafood, **Brewster Fish House** ( ☎508-896-7867; 2208 MA 6A; lunch $8-13, dinner $15-26; ☾Apr-Dec) offers spicy lobster bisque and, perhaps, scallops with sun-dried tomatoes.

# ORLEANS

### Population 6340

Orleans is often passed over by visitors in a rush to get to Provincetown, but it's definitely worth a stop. At sunset, take Main St northwest to the bayside **Rock Harbor**. Or, any time of day, take it east to the 9-mile-long **Nauset Beach** ( P$10), one of the Cape's best beaches for walking, sunning or bodysurfing. For exploring Pleasant Bay and Nauset Marsh by canoe and kayak, there's no better outfitter than the **Goose Hummock Outdoor Center** ( ☎508-255-2620; off MA 6A, Town Cove).

Most of the 47 very nice motel rooms and suites at **The Cove** ( ☎508-255-1203, 800-343-2233; www.thecoveorleans.com; 13 MA 28; d $79-189/$67-99 summer/winter) are situated right on Town Cove, but all have access to private shoreline, barbecue grills and a heated pool. The **Nauset House Inn** ( ☎508-255-2195, 800-771-5508; www.nausethouseinn.com; Beach Rd; d $65-170; ☾Apr-Oct) has friendly innkeepers, comfortable rooms, plentiful common areas (including a greenhouse conservatory) and an excellent location – it's about a 10-minute walk to Nauset Beach.

Locals and tourists alike flock to fun, informal **Land Ho!** ( ☎508-255-5165; 38 MA 6A; mains $9-15)  for inexpensive sandwiches, fried seafood platters, barbecue ribs, clam pie and burgers. **Cap't Cass Rock Harbor Seafood** (117 Rock Harbor Rd; lunch $6-12, dinner $10-30; ☺ mid-May–mid-Oct) is more quaint than most little harborside shacks and offers generous lobster rolls, clam chowder and daily blackboard specials. A rustic and rockin' hangout, **Joe's Beach Road Bar & Grille** ( ☎508-255-0212; 5 Beach Rd; dinner $8-17) serves creative and hearty seafood, steak, pizza, burgers, sandwiches and pasta. Keep your eyes peeled for lobster specials.

# ON THE ROAD

North of Orleans, MA 6A morphs into US 6. The **Cape Cod National Seashore** (CCNS) covers the whole eastern shoreline and more than 42 sq miles from Eastham to Provincetown. The fragile strip is renowned for pristine and virtually endless beaches, crashing waves, sandy dunes, nature trails, ponds, salt marshes and forests. Lingering on these shores will be the highlight of your trip.

Home to the Cape's oldest windmill, **Eastham** (population 5450) is quiet. Stop at **Fort Hill**, commanding a high position above the fragile Nauset Marsh. Its walking trails are short but lovely. Nearby, the **Edward Penniman House** ( ☎508-255-3421; free; call for hours) is a beautifully restored mid-19th century sea captain's house. Rent wheels ($22 a day) at **Little Capistrano Bike Shop** ( ☎508-255-6515; Salt Pond Rd; ☺ Apr-Nov), for the **bike trail** from Salt Pond to Coast Guard Beach. It traverses a dramatic salt marsh and winds through a pretty forest. For a good B&B on the Rail Trail, the **Overlook Inn** ( ☎508-255-1886, 877-255-1886; www.overlookinn.com; US 6; d $145-220/$115-170 summer/ winter) has 14 antique-filled guest rooms.

Heading into **Wellfleet** (population 2700), which lures visitors with art galleries, scenic roads and famous Wellfleet oysters, the easterly marsh views are downright breathtaking. For quietude, nothing beats the Audubon Society's 1000-acre **Wellfleet Bay Wildlife Sanctuary** ( ☎508-349-2615; US 6; adult/child $3/2; ☺ trails sunrise-sunset). From Wellfleet center, continue west along Main Street to Chequessett Neck Rd for the 8-mile **Great Island Trail**. For a cool beachside hangout, nothing compares to the **Beachcomber** ( ☎508-349-6055; www.thebeachcomber.com; Cahoon Hollow Beach; cover varies; ☺seasonally), an indoor-outdoor joint with live music. Or, for an unforgettably nostalgic treat, see a movie at the **Wellfleet Drive-In** ( ☎508-349-7176; US 6; ☺seasonally) at dusk.

The homey and comfy **Blue Gateways** ( ☎508-349-7530; www .bluegateways.com; 252 Main St; d $100-140/$90-110 summer/off-season; ☺ May-Oct) has three tidy guest rooms in the center of town. For large portions of very fresh seafood served at indoor picnic tables, **Moby Dick's** ( ☎508-349-9795; US 6; dishes $8-20; ☺ seasonally) has no equal.

In **Truro** (population 2100), take any winding road east or west of US 6, get lost a bit and soak in the distinct, hilly scenery. Highland Light, also known as **Cape Cod Light**, in North Truro, sits adjacent to the Cape's oldest public golf course. The **Pilgrim Heights Area** has two short trails with splendidly expansive views. One trail leads to the where the Pilgrims purportedly tasted their first spring water in the New World.

The 42-bed **Hostelling International, Truro** (☎508-349-3889, 800-909-4776 reservations; www.capecodhostels.org; N Pamet Rd; beds $15-19; ☼ late Jun-early Sep) abuts Ballston Beach and has a dramatic location amid dunes and marshes. For fancy picnic foods, nothing beats **Jams, Inc** (☎508-349-1616; off US 6; ☼ May–mid-Oct). **Adrian's** (☎508-487-4360; US 6; breakfast $3-8, dinner $8-23; ☼ mid-May–mid-Oct) specializes in Italian dishes.

The single most distinctive view on Cape Cod, no matter the time of day or season, comes as you crest a North Truro hill on US 6. All of a sudden, the expansive hook of shoreline bursts forth in a full panorama. From the easterly cookie-cutter cottages to the westerly Pilgrim Lake to the silhouetted monument, the shoreline never looks the same twice. I dare you to tire of it.

# PROVINCETOWN

**Population 3400, Map 5**

The Cape's most lively town, also New England's gay mecca, draws painters and writers, Portuguese-American fishermen and families. Walking down Commercial St you'll encounter cross-dressers, children eating saltwater taffy, leather-clad motorcyclists, barely clad inline skaters, women strolling hand in hand and unwitting tourists wondering what they've stumbled into. This is also the Cape's best town for shopping and art buying. Stop at the **chamber of commerce** (☎508-487-3424; www.ptownchamber.com; 307 Commercial St, MacMillan Wharf).

## SIGHTS & ACTIVITIES

### PROVINCETOWN ART ASSOCIATION & MUSEUM
☎508-487-1750; www.paam.org; 460 Commercial St; adult/child $5/free; ☼ late May-Sep, weekends only Oct-late May

Provincetown began attracting artists in the early 1900s, and this place, organized in 1914, became the repository for much of their work. One of the country's foremost small museums, PAAM exhibits from the permanent collection and from changing shows highlighting emerging local artists.

### PILGRIM MONUMENT & PROVINCETOWN MUSEUM
☎508-487-1310; High Pole Rd; adult/child $7/3; ☼ 9am-7pm Jul-Aug, 9am-5pm Apr-Jun & Sep-Nov

After climbing to the top of the monument for great views, pop inside to learn about the Pilgrims' struggle to survive here and about the whaling captains who later settled here.

### ART'S DUNE TOURS

☎508-487-1950; cnr Commercial & Standish Sts; $12-16; ☯ mid-Apr–mid-Nov

If you only do one or two things in Provincetown, this hour-long, narrated, 4WD dune tour within the CCNS should be one of them.

### BIKING

Seven miles of great paved bike trails crisscross the CCNS. Rent bicycles ($3/14 hour/day) at **Galeforce Bicycle & Beach Market** (☎508-487-4849; 144 Bradford St Ext).

# SLEEPING

### DUNE'S EDGE CAMPGROUND

☎508-487-9815; US 6; sites from $28; ☯ May-Sep

True to its name, this campground has 120 pine-shaded sites on the dune's edge.

### FAIRBANKS INN

☎508-487-0386, 800-324-7265; www.fairbanksinn.com; 90 Bradford St; d $129-289/$69-169 summer/winter

A gracious and historic 18th-century hostelry, the Fairbanks is arguably the friendliest place to stay in town. It boasts restored wide-pine floors and fireplaces, and its 15 rooms have been upgraded with fine amenities and down comforters. It has a central location and a tranquil back patio.

### WHITE HORSE INN

☎508-487-1790; 500 Commercial St; d $90-140/$60-100 summer/winter

Twelve basic rooms, most with shared bath, are decorated with original local art, but the six bungalow-style apartments are far more interesting and bohemian.

### COPPER FOX

☎508-487-8583; www.copperfox.net; 448 Commercial St; d $145-205/$85-100 summer/winter

Set back from the street by a lovely front yard, this renovated B&B has three rooms, two suites and two apartments with private entrances.

---

## Best Outer Cape Beaches

**Coast Guard Beach**, CCNS, Eastham; backed by undulating dune grasses
**Nauset Light Beach**, CCNS, Eastham; the stuff of dreams
**Corn Hill Beach**, bayside, Truro; a town beach nice for walking
**Head of the Meadow Beach**, CCNS, Truro; a wide, dune-backed beach great for watching moonrises
**Race Point Beach**, CCNS, Provincetown; known for its pounding surf
**Herring Cove Beach**, CCNS, Provincetown; great for watching sunsets and popular among lesbians

## Whale-watching

Of the various companies departing from MacMillan Wharf, the **Dolphin Fleet Whale Watch** ( ☎508-349-1900, 800-826-9300; adult/senior/child $19/17/16; ☾ mid-Apr–Oct, weather permitting) offers the best tours. If you've never seen these behemoths breaking the surface of the water in open ocean, you're in for a real treat. Onboard scientists and naturalists hail from the Center for Coastal Studies.

# EATING & ENTERTAINMENT

### SPIRITUS PIZZA
☎508-487-2808; 190 Commercial St; ☾ Apr–mid-Nov

Perfect for cruising and noshing, the scene at Spiritus is sure spirited. Everyone hangs here after the bars and clubs close for a late-night slice.

### BUBALA'S BY THE BAY
☎508-487-0773, 183 Commercial St; breakfast $4-9, lunch $7-15, dinner $7-26; ☾ May-Oct

If the food matched the people-watching, you'd never get a table. Keep it simple with omelets and burgers and check out the streetside parade.

### NAPI'S
☎508-487-1145; 7 Freeman St; lunch $6-13, dinner $18-26

An institution since 1973, this eclectic place offers organic salads, stir-fry, and Portuguese linguiça. It's always lively, funky and welcoming.

### LORRAINE'S
☎508-487-6074; 133 Commercial St; dinner $15-26; ☾ mid-Apr–Oct

This cozy waterfront place features Mexican cuisine with a New England twist. Try littleneck clams in a cilantro lime broth or sea scallops with tomatillos in a green chile sauce.

### PIEDBAR
☎508-487-1527; 193A Commercial St; ☾ mid-May–mid-Oct

This predominantly women's waterfront dance club serves as the venue for hot Girl Power events on weekends.

### ATLANTIC HOUSE
☎508-487-3821; 4 Masonic Place

The 'A-House' features three distinct men's bars: leather, disco and an intimate bar with an off-season fireplace.

### CROWN & ANCHOR
☎508-487-1430; 247 Commercial St

The varied lineup of cabaret, comedians and crooners is hard to beat. If you have the chance, don't miss Kate Clinton and Suede.

# ROUTE 1

**300 MILES; 3-7 DAYS**

As the crow flies, Maine's rockbound coast is about 228 miles long. But as a boat sails, its tortuous course would cover almost 3500 miles. Bays, islands, inlets, peninsulas, isthmuses and coves make up the granite coast, along with a few stretches of sandy beach. Head down practically any of these fingers of forested land, the ones that reach inland to rocky coastlines, for a taste of real Maine. That would be the Maine of 'lobstah' and lighthouses, of coastal cruises and kayaking.

To be sure, US 1 links the best the coast offers, but you'll have to get off it and head 'downeast' to get far from the madding crowds. The southern coast is by far the most thickly populated. The settlements here vary from well-preserved historic villages and genteel summer resorts to 'factory outlet' towns and honky-tonk beach towns.

But midcoast Maine is the stuff of Winslow Homer watercolors – complete with boulder-strewn coastlines, battering North Atlantic surf and merciless fog. Get as far as Bar Harbor and Mount Desert Island, deservedly hugely popular destinations, and you'll have to deal with humanity again. But there's a reason everyone comes this far. Mountains lap the sea, outdoor activities are practically endless, and back roads lead to the freshest lobster you'll ever consume.

From Boston, take I-93 north to I-95 north, through a sliver of seacoast New Hampshire (where I-95 becomes the New Hampshire turnpike, a toll road) and cross the Piscataqua River into Kittery (60 miles; 1¼ hours). Along the south coast, where roads flood with summer traffic, US 1 parallels I-95 (aka Maine Turnpike, a toll road). Beyond Freeport, I-95 cuts inland while US 1 hugs the coastline. This is where things start thinning out a bit, where 'Maine, the way life should be' gets more interesting. Accordingly, plan for more driving time in Maine.

# ON THE ROAD

**Kittery** (population 4900) can be less than thrilling, unless you're shopping. It's famous for malls and outlet stores, all of which are strewn along US 1 and claim to offer deep discounts. If shopping isn't your bag, keep going. US 1 from Kittery to Portland is the coastal Maine's commercial artery, lined with motels, campgrounds, gas stations, restaurants and shops.

York Village, York Harbor and York Beach make up the **Yorks** (population 12,850). **York Village**, chartered in 1641, has a well-preserved village center of colonial buildings. The **Old York Historical Society** ( ☎207-363-4974; www.oldyork.org; family/adult/child $15/7/3; 🕙10am-5pm Tue-Sat, 1-5pm Sun mid-Jun–Sep) has preserved several of them as a museum of town history. **York Harbor** was developed more than a century ago as a posh summer resort, and it still maintains some of that feeling today. The working-class roots of **York Beach** still show in its large number of RV parks and humdrum commercial development. Families may want to visit the state's largest zoo, **York's Wild Kingdom** ( ☎207-363-4911, 800-456-4911; US 1; adult/child $12.50/8.25; ☺Memorial Day–mid-Sep).

# OGUNQUIT

## Population 1200

This family-friendly 'Beautiful Place by the Sea,' known for its 3-mile sand beach, affords swimmers the choice of chilly, pounding surf or warm, peaceful back-cove waters. It's also a gay and lesbian mecca. Ogunquit stretches down Shore Rd to **Perkins Cove** (a little spit of land inundated with shops and tourists) and to neighboring **Wells** (population 9400). Despite good beaches, Wells is dismaying, a visual assault perpetrated by American commercial-strip development. Contact the **Ogunquit Welcome Center** ( ☎207-646-5533; US 1) for more information.

Take **Marginal Way**, Ogunquit's well-known coastline footpath, which starts near Beach St at Shore Rd and ends near Perkins Cove. The mile-long right-of-way follows the sea's scenic 'margin,' hence its name. **Ogunquit Beach** (or Main Beach to locals) is only a five-minute walk along aptly named Beach St, east of US 1. For cruising, the lobster boat **Finestkind** ( ☎207-646-5227; Perkins Cove; adult/child $11/7; ☺9am-6pm late Apr–mid-Oct, weather permitting) takes passengers on 50-minute voyages to pull traps and collect these delicious crustaceans. Taste one later at the **Lobster Shack** ( ☎207-646-2941; 110 Perkins Cove Rd; mains $6-18; ☺seasonally). In business since 1947, the Shack serves the cheapest lobster and steamers in town.

For a truly extraordinary dining experience, **Arrows** ( ☎207-361-1100; Berwick Rd; mains $37-42; ☺dinner mid-Apr–mid-Dec), located in a beautifully restored 18th-century farmhouse, never disappoints. The chef-owners hail from San Francisco, where they absorbed Asian influences. Try the grilled lobster stewed in a Thai-style curry sauce. Make reservations! Drive 4 miles west of Ogunquit on Berwick Rd.

Staying overnight? **The West Highland Inn** ( ☎207-646-2181; www.westhighlandinn.com; 38 Shore Rd; d $70-145; ☺mid-May–mid-Oct) is a centrally located Victorian summer house with 14 rooms. Gay- and lesbian-friendly **Moon Over Maine** ( ☎207-646-6666, 800-851-6837; www.moonovermaine.com; 22 Berwick Rd; d $79-129; ☺mid-May–mid-Oct) has nine rooms in a 1839 Cape-style house and an outdoor hot tub.

# THE KENNEBUNKS

## Population 4800

The Kennebunks are comprised of Kennebunk, Kennebunkport and Kennebunk Beach. **Kennebunkport** has pristine 100- and 200-year-old houses and mansions, manicured lawns and sea views. Although it's packed in the summer, even in the autumn visitors throng here to boutique shop, sleep in gracious inns and drive the dramatic **Ocean Ave**, which eventually leads to **Walkers Point** and the Bush compound (the vacation residence of former president George Bush). It's not all that exciting, but every visitor to Kennebunkport makes the drive to stare at the black Secret Service vehicles. Continue northeast on Ocean Ave to reach **Cape Porpoise**, a charming hamlet. The historic district of Kennebunkport is south of **Dock Square** (the town's epicenter). The **chamber of commerce** ( ☎207-967-0857; www.kkcc.maine.org; ME 9) is located in Kennebunk Lower Village.

Bicycling is a good way to get around Kennebunkport. And the ultra-capable **Bike Shop** ( ☎207-967-4382, 800-220-0907; 83 Arundel Rd; ☉10am-5pm Mon-Sat mid-Mar–Oct) obliges with rentals ($12/18 3 hrs/day); follow North St from Dock Square.

# SLEEPING & EATING

### SALTY ACRES CAMPGROUND
☎207-967-2483; ME 9; sites $22-25; ☉mid-May–mid-Oct

This family-friendly, modestly developed campground has 225 sites near Cape Porpoise and is less than a mile to Goose Rocks Beach. Choose between sunny and wooded sites, some of which are close to the pool.

### GREEN HERON INN
☎207-967-3315; www.greenheroninn.com; 126 Ocean Ave; d $99-175; ☉Mar–mid-Oct

This dependably comfy inn has 11 rooms with TV and air-conditioning. Pet-friendly rooms are available for an additional $10 a day.

### THE CAPTAIN LORD MANSION
☎207-967-3141; www.captainlord.com; 6 Pleasant St; d $199-369

When money is no object, this meticulously restored sea captain's house is without competition. It's probably more plush and beautiful now than when lived in by its original occupants.

### THE CLAM SHACK
☎207-967-2560; 3 Western Ave; dishes $3-13; ☉seasonally

Next to the Kennebunk Lower Village bridge, this white shack doles out burgers, fried clams and fish plates. If you eat overlooking the water, beware of seagulls snatching your food.

### FEDERAL JACK'S RESTAURANT & BREW PUB
☎207-967-4322; 8 Western Ave; dishes $6-15

In the Shipyard complex in Kennebunk Lower Village, Federal Jack's boasts good pub grub and some heartier main courses. Their microbrews are excellent, as are the downstairs 'handcrafted' drafts.

### WHITE BARN INN
☎207-967-2321; www.whitebarninn.com; 37 Beach St; 4-course dinner $77; ☉6-9:30pm Mon-Thu, 5:30-9:30pm Fri-Sun (closed most of Jan)

Kennebunkport's most renowned New American restaurant, thick with 'country-elegant' decor and ambiance, is worth a special-occasion splurge. The menu changes weekly and features local seafood complemented by locally grown herbs, fruits and vegetables and California greens. Make reservations and don your finest attire.

# ON THE ROAD

**Old Orchard Beach** (population 8850), the quintessential Maine beach playground, is saturated with skimpily clad crowds of fun-loving sun worshippers making the rounds of fast-food emporiums, mechanical amusements and trinket shops. **Palace Playland**, on the beach at the very center of town, is a fitting symbol, with its carousel, Ferris wheel, children's rides, pizza and fried clam stands, and T-shirt and souvenir shops.

Just off ME 207, Cape Elizabeth plays host to **Fort Williams Park**, worth visiting for panoramic and picnic possibilities. Adjacent to the park, **Portland Head Light** is the oldest of Maine's 52 functioning lighthouses. It was commissioned by President George Washington in 1791 and staffed until 1989. The keeper's house is now the **Museum at Portland Head Light** ( ☎207-799-2661; www.portlandheadlight.com; adult/child $2/1; ☷10am-4pm daily Jun–mid-Oct; 10am-4pm weekends Apr, May, mid-Oct–mid-Dec).

# PORTLAND

## Population 64,250

A small, manageable, safe and prosperous place, Portland is Maine's largest city, port and commercial center. It's a great place to linger or to live. Rife with cobblestone streets, brick buildings and gas lanterns, the **Old Port** section begs for exploration and rewards with excellent restaurants, cafes and shops. It's particularly romantic and moody by twilight. To reach the Old Port follow I-95 to I-295 to US 1 to US 1A North, (aka Commercial St) where you'll find the **Convention & Visitors Bureau** ( ☎207-772-5800; www.visitportland.com; 305 Commercial St).

## SIGHTS & ACTIVITIES

### PORTLAND MUSEUM OF ART

☎207-775-6148; www.portlandmuseum.org; 7 Congress Square; adult/senior/child $8/6/2; ☷10am-5pm Tue-Sun, 10am-9pm Fri (& 10am-5pm Mon mid-May–mid-Oct)

These outstanding collections are especially rich in works by Maine painters Winslow Homer, Edward Hopper, Rockwell Kent and Andrew Wyeth. But the PMA also has the works of European masters like Degas, Picasso and Renoir.

### CHILDREN'S MUSEUM OF MAINE
☎207-828-1234; 142 Free St; over age 1 yr $6 ⏱10am-5pm Mon-Sat, noon-5pm Sun (closed Mon in winter)
Give the kids an opportunity to haul in lobster traps on a childsize boat, broadcast the news and make stained glass. They'll thank you for it.

### SEA KAYAKING
Casco Bay islands make an ideal destination for sea kayaking. Take a 15-minute ferry ride with **Casco Bay Lines** (☎207-774-7871; www.cascobaylines.com; 56 Commercial St; adult/child $6/3) to Peaks Island and then hook up with **Maine Island Kayak Company** (☎207-766-2373, 800-796-2373; 70 Luther St), a reputable outfitter offering daily instruction and tours.

### CRUISES
**Casco Bay Lines** also cruises the islands delivering mail, freight and visitors. Although these are working boats, they're comfortably outfitted. Five of the six scenic cruises operate daily year-round, and they vary from 1¾ hours to 5¾ hours (adult/senior/child from $11/9/5). All cruises depart from the Maine State Pier.

# SLEEPING

Several moderately priced motels are located at I-95 exit 8, including **Comfort Inn** (☎800-228-5150; d off-season/in-season from $69/129), **Portland Marriott** (☎207-871-8000; d off-season/in-season from $89/$200) and **Days Inn** (☎207-772-3450; d off-season/in-season from $62/$124).

### PORTLAND REGENCY HOTEL
☎207-774-4200, 800-727-3436; www.theregency.com; 20 Milk St; d $159-229
Portland's most upscale hotel, smack in the middle of the Old Port, has 95 rooms housed in a substantial red-brick armory.

### POMEGRANATE INN
☎207-772-1006, 800-356-0408; www.pomegranateinn.com; 49 Neal St; d $115-255
Portland's West End is a quiet, mostly red brick residential neighborhood with many grand Victorian houses, some of which have been converted to inns. Few innkeepers can mix modern art with antiques as skillfully as Isabel Smiles has done here. An antiques dealer and interior designer, Smiles's eclectic taste runs the gamut from faux marble columns in the living room to hand-painted walls and century-old dressers in the eight guest rooms. Large contemporary sculpture and collages are displayed in the hallways.

### INN ON CARLETON
☎207-775-1910, 800-639-1779; www.innoncarleton.com; 46 Carleton St; d $119-199
This restored West Ender, an 1869 Victorian, has six grandiose rooms, all with massive antique headboards and period furniture.

# EATING

## BECKY'S DINER
☎207-773-7070; 390 Commercial St; dishes $3-12; ☺4am-9pm

For mingling with working fisherfolk, there's no better place than this waterfront diner. Sit at the counter with the salty dogs and order morning muffins or afternoon sandwiches.

## PEPPERCLUB
☎207-772-0531; 78 Middle St; dinner $8-14

The main draws here are reasonably priced veggie fare served by a friendly waitstaff. The eclectic menu might include Thai lime vegetables with udon noodles or mushroom and fresh basil lasagna.

## STREET & CO
☎207-775-0887, 33 Wharf St; dinner $16-27

The menu might be simple but the Street's seafood is Portland's freshest. There's grilled, broiled or Cajun-style fish (tuna, salmon, swordfish), plus various sea critters like mussels, clams and calamari served steamed or sautéed. Have your choice served over pasta or in a broth perfect for dipping with a hunk of fresh bread. The cramped but congenial dining rooms are usually packed, so reserve in advance.

## FORE STREET
☎207-775-2717; 288 Fore St; dinner $15-25

If you have just one night in Portland, dine at Fore. The airy, exposed-brick and pine-panel room features an open-air kitchen where chef-owner Sam Hayward works utter magic. Applewood grilling and roasting are his forte, and, whenever possible, he uses local meats. Start with roasted Blue Hill bay mussels with pistachios; move to tender roasted pork loin; and save room for maple crème brûlée.

# FREEPORT

## Population 1800

Forget US 1 for a minute; hop on I-95 to Freeport, where you'll encounter a perpetual traffic jam. Amid the natural beauties of Maine's rockbound central coast, Freeport is devoted almost entirely to city-style shopping. Tony luggage, expensive china, trendy clothes and perfumed soaps are all available in more than 100 shops. In summer, outdoorsy outfitter **LL Bean** (☎800-341-4341; Main St; ☺24hr), and indeed most of Freeport's shops, is busy with shoppers all day and into the night. The **chamber of commerce** (☎207-865-1212; www.freeportusa.com; Main St) can help with more details.

# ON THE ROAD

You're now entering midcoast Maine, the section celebrated for exceptional natural beauty and down-to-earth residents. Expect dramatic coastlines dotted with friendly seaside villages, thick pine forests and lots of biking, hiking, sailing and kayaking possibilities.

In **Brunswick** (population 14,800), where I-95 and US 1 diverge, US 1 heads northeast along the coast. Home of highly regarded **Bowdoin College**, the town is filled with Federal and Greek mansions built by wealthy sea captains. At 63 Federal St, Harriet Beecher Stowe wrote *Uncle Tom's Cabin*.

Just up the road, as early as 1607, wooden ships were built and launched in **Bath** (population 9260). Today, it's still one of the country's largest shipyards: **Bath Iron Works** (BIW) builds steel frigates, cruisers and other navy craft. Bath's biggest attraction, the **Maine Maritime Museum & Shipyard** (☎207-443-1316; 243 Washington St; adult/senior/child $9.75/8.75/6.75; ☯9:30am-5pm) preserves the Kennebec's long shipbuilding tradition. Don't overlook the Historic District, with long stretches of 19th-century Victorian homes. Bath's attractive, small commercial district is north of US 1, centered on Front St.

Bath has many reasonably priced B&Bs in nice 19th-century houses, including the **Inn at Bath** (☎207-443-4294, 800-423-0964; www.innatbath.com; 969 Washington St; r $115-185 in season, $75-165 Nov-Apr), easily Bath's most splendid hostelry. You can expect plenty of antiques in these nine rooms. As for eats, at the downtown **Beale Street Grill** (☎207-442-9514, 215 Water St; mains $8-14; ☯11am-9pm) happy patrons gnaw on baby back ribs while downing Maine microbrews.

**Wiscasset's** (population 1200) history as a major 19th-century shipbuilding port has left a legacy of exceptionally grand and beautiful houses, many of which have been converted into thriving antiques stores. Wiscasset's grandest and best-situated mansion, **Castle Tucker** (☎207-882-7169; cnr High & Lee Sts; $5; ☯11am-5pm Fri-Sun Jun–mid-Oct), commands beautiful views whether or not you tour it. For picnicking, there's no better place than the 1808 **Fort Edge-comb** (☎207-882-7777; 66 Fort Rd, North Edgecomb; $1), a half-mile

## Got Boots?

Freeport's fame and fortune began a century ago when Leon Leonwood Bean opened a shop to sell equipment and provisions to hunters and fishermen heading into the Maine woods. LL Bean gave good value for the money, and his customers were loyal. One foundation of their loyalty was his Maine Hunting Shoe, a rugged rubber bottom molded to a leather upper. It kept hunters' feet dry and warm as they crouched in their duck blinds at dawn.

Over the years, the LL Bean retail store grew into a 24/7/365 operation (the store never closes) and has an iron-clad returns policy: send anything back, any time, if it proves unsatisfactory.

south of the eastern end of the bridge that spans the **Sheepscot River**. Almost everyone stops at **Red's Eats** (Main St; dishes $1-13; ☽May-Sep), a simple little red take-out stand. Since the 1940s, it's served Maine's tastiest clam and whole-lobster rolls.

The twin towns of **Newcastle** (population 1750) and **Damariscotta** (population 2040), pretty Maine towns with numerous churches and attractive commercial districts, basically serve the smaller communities of the southerly Pemaquid Peninsula.

Be sure to detour off US 1 to ME 130 south through the juicy heart of the Pemaquid Peninsula to gorgeous **Pemaquid Point**. Artists flock here to capture the beauty of the tortuous, grainy igneous rock formations pounded by restless, treacherous seas. Perched atop the rocks the 1827 **Pemaquid Light** (adult $2, child under 12 yrs & senior free) is but one of Maine's 61 surviving lighthouses. Stop at the reconstructed **Fort William Henry** ( ☎207-677-2423; adult/child $1/free; ☽9am-5pm late May-Aug) for commanding ocean views.

**Rockland** (population 7600), the 'Lobster Capital of the World', is, along with Camden, the center of Maine's very busy windjammer sailing business. Do stop because of the **Farnsworth Art Museum & Wyeth Center** ( ☎207-596-6457; www.farnsworthmuseum.org; 16 Museum St; adult/student $8/4; ☽9am-5pm late May–mid-Oct, 10am-5pm Tue-Sat, 1-5pm Sun mid-Oct–late May), one of the country's best small regional museums. Its collection is especially strong in the works of the Wyeths, Louise Nevelson, Rockwell Kent, John Marin and others. Also noteworthy, two miles south of Rockland on ME 73, is the **Owls Head Transportation Museum** ( ☎207-594-4418; www.ohtm.org; ME 73, Owls Head; adult/child 5-12 yrs/family $7/5/18; ☽10am-5pm Apr-Oct, 10am-4pm Nov-Mar). The museum collects, preserves (yes, everything works!) and exhibits pioneer (pre-1920) aircraft, vehicles and engines that were instrumental in the evolution of transportation as we know it today.

For overnighting in Rockland, the **LimeRock Inn** ( ☎207-594-2257, 800-546-3762; www.limerockinn.com; 96 Limerock St; d $105-215), an eight-room mansion built in 1890, is decorated with fine mahogany furniture. **Primo** ( ☎207-596-0770; 2 S Main St/ME

## Lighting the Way

These lighthouses are worth searching out.
**Cape Neddick Light** (Nubble Light), off US 1A, York Beach
**Cape Elizabeth Light**, off ME 77, South Portland
**Portland Head Light**, off Cape Elizabeth, Portland
**Pemaquid Light**, off ME 130, Pemaquid Point
**Owl's Head Light**, off ME 73, south of Rockland
**Dice Head Light**, off ME 166, Castine
**Bass Harbor Head Light**, off ME 102, Bass Harbor (Mt Desert)
**Bear Light**, offshore from Northeast Harbor (Mt Desert)

73; dinner $12-22; ☺Jul-Sep, Thu-Sun Oct-Jun) happens when an award-winning chef marries an award-winning baker and pastry chef. The bistro, ensconced in a Victorian home and one of the region's top restaurants, features creative veal, lamb and seafood dishes. Make reservations a month in advance.

# CAMDEN

## Population 3950

Camden's picturesque harbor, shadowed by the mountains of Camden Hills State Park, is one of the prettiest sites in the state. Period. Home to Maine's famed fleet of windjammers, Camden is also popular with J Crew catalog–type landlubbers. The **chamber of commerce** (☎207-236-4404; www.camdenme.org) is on the waterfront.

## SIGHTS & ACTIVITIES

### CAMDEN HILLS STATE PARK
☎207-236-3109; adult/child $2/50¢

Just north on US 1, the park yields up exquisite views of Penobscot Bay. It also has an extensive system of well-marked hiking trails, from the half-mile, 45-minute climb up **Mt Battie** to the 3-mile, two-hour Ski Shelter Trail. Simple trail maps are available at the park entrance. The picnic area also has short trails down to the shore.

### SEA KAYAKING
For paddling, contact **Maine Sport Outfitters** (☎800-722-0826; Harbor Park, US 1), which offers rentals ($50/65 daily per single/tandem) and two-hour tours of Camden Harbor ($45).

### BICYCLING
Drive 5 miles to Lincolnville Beach, then board a 20-minute ferry (☎207-789-5611, call for schedule) to **Islesboro**, one of the Maine's finest places to ride. The island is relatively flat, yet hilly enough to offer majestic vistas of Penobscot Bay and to feature a 28-mile bike loop. Rent bikes ($17 a day) at **Ragged Mountain Sports** (☎207-236-6664; 46 Elm St, Camden).

## SLEEPING & EATING

### CAMDEN HILLS STATE PARK
☎207-236-3109; US 1; sites $15-20; ☺mid-May–mid-Oct

This park has hot showers, flush toilets and 107 forested campsites without hookups. A few sites are held on a first-come, first-served basis, but you'll have to arrive by noon to claim one of these.

### BLUE HARBOR HOUSE
☎207-236-3196, 800-248-3196; www.blueharborhouse.com; 67 Elm St; d $115-205; ☺May-Oct

This cozy Cape Cod–style house (1810) has 10 guest rooms and amicable owners.

### BLACKBERRY INN
☎207-236-6060, 800-388-6000; www.blackberryinn.com; 82 Elm St; d $99-245
A gorgeous Victorian with high ceilings, most of these fully restored eight rooms have vintage tin ceilings and fireplaces. Ask about the spacious family-friendly efficiency.

### CAPPY'S
☎207-236-2254; 1 Main St; dishes $5-15; 11am-9pm
Many places in Maine bill themselves as 'the place for chowder,' but this one's probably telling the truth. Get a huge mug of thick, creamy chowder – chock-full of clams and potatoes – served with a buttermilk biscuit.

### FROGWATER CAFE & BAKERY
☎207-236-8998; 31 Elm St; lunch & dinner $10-18; mid-Apr–mid-Nov
Vegetarian and sweet freaks will leap for veggie shepherd's pie and cinnamon bread pudding.

### ATLANTICA
☎207-236-6011; Bay View Landing; lunch $7-14, dinner $15-24 call for times
Chef-owned Atlantica serves Camden's best seafood alongside good bay views. Try the pan-seared peppered tuna or the sautéed gingered scallops.

# ON THE ROAD

Just north of Camden near **Belfast** (population 6400) and **Searsport** (population 1100), US 1 is lined with dozens of motels, campgrounds, restaurants, antique shops and flea markets. These dining, lodging and shopping opportunities are considerably cheaper, and more likely to have vacancies in the summer, than those in Camden and Bar Harbor. Contact **Waldo County** ( ☎800-870-9934; www.waldocountymaine.com) for hotel and restaurant recommendations.

A crossroads for highways and rail lines, **Bucksport** (population 2970) is a workaday town with light industry and a big paper mill. Look a little closer, though, and you'll also find an artsy community. Just north of the bridge on ME 174, the huge granite **Fort Knox State Historic Site** ( ☎207-469-7719; adult/child $2/50¢; 9am-sunset summer, 9am-6:30pm spring & fall) dominates the Penobscot River and was garrisoned during the Civil War and the Spanish-American War. There's a nice picnic area outside the admissions gate.

Continue north on US 1 to **Ellsworth** (population 6450), a necessary commercial area that serves the region, where you'll head south on ME 3 for **Mount Desert Island**, the grand prize for coming so far. This is where mountains of spruce forests rush to meet fjordlike fingers of deep water. Coastal vistas reach far into

These grand sailing vessels take happy passengers out into Penobscot Bay. In Camden hop aboard the **Appledore** ( ☎207-236-8353; $25 per adult) for an unforgettable two-hour cruise. The schooner **Wendameen** ( ☎207-594-1751; $180 per person) takes passengers cruising overnight. For three- to six-day cruises ($350 to $850 per person), contact the **Maine Windjammer Association** ( ☎207-374-2955, 800-807-9463; www.sailmainecoast.com).

the horizon. Visitors are explicably drawn to hike 120 miles of trails, bike 58 miles of unpaved carriage roads and camp at 500-plus campsites. Mt Desert Island (pronounced duh-*zert*) holds **Bar Harbor** (Maine's oldest and most popular summer resort), numerous delightful seaside villages, the windswept granite summit of Cadillac Mountain and most of **Acadia National Park**. **Hulls Cove Visitor Center** ( ☎207-288-3338; ME 3; ♥May-Oct), 16 miles south of Ellsworth, and the **Acadia Information Center** ( ☎207-667-8550, 800-358-8550; www.acadiainfo.com; ME 3; ♥May-Oct) are good sources. Before heading into Bar Harbor, stop at the **Trenton Bridge Lobster Pound** ( ☎207-667-2977; ME 3, Ellsworth; prices $9-20; ♥May–mid-Oct), the oldest and best of the lobster pounds.

# BAR HARBOR

### Population 2680

Chartered in 1796, Bar Harbor rivaled Newport, Rhode Island for the stature of its summer-colony guests by the end of the 19th century. Although a vast forest fire in 1947 torched 60 palatial 'summer cottages' of wealthy summer residents, putting an end to Bar Harbor's gilded age, it soon recovered as a destination for common folk who love the outdoors. The **Bar Harbor Chamber of Commerce** ( ☎207-288-5103, 800-345-4617; www.barharborinfo.com) maintains a small information office at the Bar Harbor Town Pier in the summer; otherwise, head to 93 Cottage St.

## SIGHTS & ACTIVITIES

### BAR HARBOR BICYCLE SHOP

☎207-288-3886; 141 Cottage St; rentals $19 daily, $106 weekly

In the early 20th century John Rockefeller Jr developed an incredible network of gravel carriage roads around Acadia National Park intended for horse-drawn carriage rides. Now, in the early 21st century, they prove perfectly suited for mountain bike touring. Great maps, as well as locks and helmets, are included with rentals here.

### NATIONAL PARK CANOE RENTALS

☎207-244-5854; Long Pond, off ME 102 near Somesville; ☺late May–mid-Oct

Canoeing and kayaking around the protected Long Pond is an easy way to appreciate the drama of the area. This outfitter also offers open sea tours and paddles around the dramatic Somes Sound.

### DOWNEAST WINDJAMMER AND LIGHTHOUSE CRUISES

☎207-288-4585, 288-2373; Bar Harbor Inn Pier; adult/child $29.50/19.50

As for cruising, getting out on Frenchman Bay will be an absolute highlight. Don't miss the two-hour cruise aboard the majestic 151ft, four-masted schooner *Margaret Todd*.

### BAR HARBOR WHALE WATCH CO

☎207-288-2386, 800-508-1499; 1 West St; adult/child 5-15 yrs/child under 5 yrs $45/25/8

Docked next to the pier, this outfit offers 3½- to 4-hour cruises that go in search of whales, puffins and lighthouses. It's really a very good trip (only offered from mid-May to mid-October), and an onboard naturalist provides interesting commentary.

### ATLANTIC CLIMBING

☎207-288-2521; 24 Cottage St; $100/180 half/full day

Acadia National Park, bathed in granite, is a rock climbing mecca, and the folks here offer guided trips and instructional services.

### ABBE MUSEUM

☎207-288-3519; 26 Mt Desert St; adult/child $6/2; ☺10am-5pm daily mid-May–mid-Oct, 10am-5pm Thurs-Sun mid-Oct–mid-May

There's no finer place for a nice introduction to the culture of local Wabanaki Native Americans than this spanking-new museum. The 10,000-year timeline is artfully done.

# SLEEPING & EATING

Bar Harbor has more than 2500 guest rooms, but you'll have trouble finding one in August without reservations. The **chamber of commerce** ( ☎207-288-5103; www.visitbarharbor.com) can help. For camping, contact the Hulls Cover Visitor Center (p39).

### THE VILLAGER MOTEL

☎207-288-3211; 207 Main St; d $60-138; ☺mid-May–late Oct

Run by a 10th-generation Bar Harbor family, this spic-and-span motel is a block south of the town green.

### BASS COTTAGE

☎207-288-3705; 14 The Field; d $60-100; ☺mid-May–late Oct

Hidden from the masses, this 'cottage' has 10 simple rooms, some with shared bath, on a late 19th-century Victorian estate.

## THE LEDGELAWN INN

☎207-288-4596; www.barharborvacations.com; 66 Mt Desert St; d $95-275; ☼mid-May–late Oct

Bar Harbor's most magnificent downtown inn, this vast Colonial-Revival 'summer cottage' dates to 1904. Exuding charm and grandeur, it's yours for a price, which, by the way, includes afternoon tea.

## COACH STOP INN

☎207-288-9886; www.coachstopinn.com; ME 3, Hulls Cove; d $59-139; ☼mid-May–late Oct

Just 2 miles from the main entrance to Acadia, this five-room inn, built in 1804, is set on 3 acres of gardens.

## CAFE THIS WAY

☎207-288-4483; 14-1/2 Mt Desert St; breakfast $4-12, dinner $9-15; ☼May–mid-Oct

Casual and quirky, this is *the* place for Maine blueberry pancakes or eggs Benedict with smoked trout. Sit back, listen to smooth jazz, peruse one of the many books and chow down. It also serves fresh seafood dinners.

## LOMPOC CAFE

☎207-288-9392; 36 Rodick St; dishes $6-13; ☼11:30am-3pm & 5-9:30pm mid-May–late Oct

The short but eclectic, international menu – Indonesian peanut chicken, shrimp étouffée and ingenious pizzas – is topped off with Bar Harbor Real Ale. For the intrepid, there's also blueberry ale. Most evenings feature live entertainment.

## REEL PIZZA CINERAMA

☎207-288-3828; 33B Kennebec St; pizza $9-15

Reel Pizza caters to those who like munching on good pizza, drinking local beer, slouching on couches and watching nightly flicks ($5).

## CAFE BLUEFISH

☎207-288-3696; 122 Cottage St; dinner $17-27

This intimate storefront bistro prepares tasty seafood like pecan-crusted salmon and Cajun crusted swordfish, but, strangely, no bluefish.

# ACADIA NATIONAL PARK

Acadia National Park, New England's only national park, covers more than 62 sq miles. In fact, it covers the majority (but not all) of the land on Mount Desert Island. It also includes tracts of land on the Schoodic Peninsula south of Winter Harbor and on Isle au Haut, far to the southwest.

In 1901 wealthy summer residents began donating land to a newly formed land trust, which, by 1919, became a national park. The largest donor, giving 10,000 acres, was John D Rockefeller Jr. Alarmed at the prospect of the park being overrun with automobiles, he ordered construction of 58 miles of one-lane, gravel-topped carriage roads throughout the park. The carriage roads were to provide access to the park's more remote areas by horse-drawn carriage rather than automobile. Today, these roads are deservedly popular with hikers and mountain bikers.

The park's admission fee ($10 per vehicle, $2 per bike) is good for seven consecutive days. The visitor center is located at park's main entrance at Hulls Cove, northwest of Bar Harbor via ME 3. From here, the 20-mile-long **Park Loop Rd** circumnavigates the northeastern section of the island. It is a one-way road for much of its length.

On the portion of Park Loop Rd called Ocean Drive, stop at **Thunder Hole**, south of the Overlook entrance, where the surf crashes into a cleft in the granite (the effect is best with a strong incoming tide). Not much further south, you'll find **Otter Cliffs**, a wall of pink granite rising right from the sea.

At **Jordan Pond**, where you can take a worthy self-guided nature trail, you'll be in the midst of the trail and carriage road system. Stop at the magnificently sited **Jordan Pond House** (☎207-276-3116; Park Loop Rd, Seal Harbor; tea $7; ☀mid-May–late Oct) for tea and delectable popovers with strawberry jam.

For a nice, easy hike, consider making the quick (20 minutes) ascent up **The Beehive** near the Overlook entrance; for a longer walk on the more-secluded 'backside' of the island, try the **St Saveur-Flying Mountain Loop Trail**, off Fernald Point Rd, just north of Southwest Harbor.

Swimming here is not for the faint of heart – water temperatures never reach a humane level. If you're brave, head to **Sand Beach** or **Seal Harbor** for a salty swim, or to **Echo Lake** for a fresh water dip. **Cyclists** should park near Eagle Lake, off ME 233, and pedal on the carriage paths around this body of water. Start or finish your first explorations with a stop at the windy summit of **Cadillac Mountain** (1530ft), the highest point in the park.

# ON THE ROAD

You absolutely should not miss making a circle tour of Mount Desert Island. Head out of Bar Harbor on ME 3. Just beyond Seal Harbor, the tranquil **Northeast Harbor** (population 2100) has a marina full of yachts, a main street populated with galleries and boutiques and back streets dotted with comfortable summer hideaways. The bistro **151 Main St** (☎207-276-9898; 151 Main St; dinner $8-12; ☀Tue-Sun mid-Mar–late Oct) serves the island's best food outside of Bar Harbor. Try the white clam pizza or griddled beef and pork meatloaf.

Follow ME 3/198 around Somes Sound to ME 102. Head south past Somesville and Echo Lake to **Southwest Harbor** (population 1960). More laid-back and less affluent than Northeast Harbor, it's home to the venerable **Beal's Lobster Pound** (☎207-244-3202; 1 Clark Point Rd; mains $3-15; ☀9am-8pm mid-May–mid-Oct). Grab a picnic table and dine on chowder, crabmeat rolls and, what else, lobster. Consider yourself lucky.

# KANCAMAGUS HIGHWAY

## MAP 7; NEW HAMPSHIRE                    42 MILES; 1-3 DAYS

The Kancamagus Hwy (NH 112), a beautiful wilderness road over Kancamagus Pass (2868ft), cuts through the heart of the White Mountain National Forest (WMNF), New England's greatest national forest and the largest east of the Mississippi. Although it's a heavily trafficked road, the 'Kanc' barely feels the weight. It's rarely closed, and with the exception of spring 'mud season,' there are always places to play. Naturalists disperse like scavengers at a hunt to hike, camp at rustic and backwoods site, canoe, kayak, ski, watch leaves turn color and snowshoe. There are no services on the two-lane highway, but it is bookended by service towns.

It's 2½ hours from Boston; take I-93 north to NH 112 and Lincoln/North Woodstock. To return to Boston from North Conway, head south on US 302 to NH 16 to the Spaulding Turnpike (a toll road) to I-95 to I-93.

# NORTH WOODSTOCK & LINCOLN

## Population: North Woodstock 1150; Lincoln 1270

These twin one-street towns serve a diverse clientele: outdoorsy types in heavy boots stopping for camping provisions and retirees in huge RVs stopping for cocktails after photographing roadside attractions. Just south of town, the boulder-strewn Pemigewasset River dances around the highway, providing the perfect pathway for your eyes to reach toward 360-degree mountain views. The local **chamber of commerce** ( ☎ 603-745-6621; www.lincolnwoodstock.com; NH 112, Lincoln) is helpful.

## SLEEPING & EATING

### WOODWARD'S MOTOR INN
☎ 603-745-8141, 800-635-8968; www.woodwardsresort.com; US 3, Lincoln; d from $69
Check out the facilities: an indoor pool, sauna, hot tub, racquetball court, tennis court and game room. Oh yeah: there are 85 good rooms.

### WILDERNESS INN
☎ 603-745-3890, 800-200-9453; www.thewildernessinn.com; US3 at NH 112, N Woodstock; d from $70
A former lumber mill owner's house, the inn offers lots of mahogany, congenial hosts, seven guest rooms and a separate cottage by the river.

### SUNNY DAY DINER
☎ 603-745-4833; US 3, N Woodstock; dishes $3-15; ⏱7am-2pm Thu-Mon, dinner Fri & Sat
This authentic diner serves classic fare: peanut butter and jelly sandwiches and blue-plate specials like pot roast, roast pork and salmon.

## WOODSTOCK STATION & BREWERY

☎603-745-3951; Main St, N Woodstock; mains $9-17; ☺lunch & dinner

With upwards of 150 items, from Mexican dishes and Peking ravioli to seafood and burgers, this eatery tries to be everything to everyone. In the end, it satisfies most cravings. The beer-sodden tavern is one happening joint.

# ON THE ROAD

The winding Kancamagus Hwy, portions of which were built as logging roads when the forest was heavily cut in the 19th century, is utterly unspoiled by commercial development. It offers absurdly easy access to heavily wooded, rustic **USFS campgrounds** ( ☎603-536-1310, 603-447-5448, 877-444-6777 for reservations; $16), mostly with pit toilets. Arrive in the morning to secure a site, which are first-come, first-serve; arrive on Thursday or Friday morning to get one for the weekend. Take this tip very seriously during foliage season.

As for hiking, the White Mountain National Forest (WMNF) is laced with excellent trails of varying difficulty. For detailed trail information, stop at any of the WMNF ranger stations. The most convenient is located just off I-93 at exit 32 ( ☎603-528-8721, 603-744-9165). Here you can purchase the requisite **parking permits** ($3/5/20 daily/weekly/seasonally).

Downhill skiers will appreciate **Loon Mountain** ( ☎603-745-8111; www.loonmtn.com), a family-friendly mountain with 45 trails (more than half of which are rated intermediate) and 10 lifts. Snowboarders

---

### DETOUR: FRANCONIA NOTCH

Before doing the Kanc, head north on I-93 through **Franconia Notch**, a narrow gorge shaped eons ago by a wild stream cutting through craggy granite. The dramatic mountain pass (notch) takes you to **The Flume** (adult/child $8/5; ☺9am-4:30pm daily mid-May–mid Oct), a natural cleft (12ft to 20ft wide) in the granite bedrock. Don't miss the 2-mile self-guided nature walk that leads along an 800ft boardwalk to a rushing flume of water. Hop back in the car for **The Basin**, a huge glacial pothole 20ft in diameter that was carved deep into the granite 15,000 years ago. For leaf peepers, the **Cannon Mountain Aerial Tramway** ( ☎603-823-7722; adult/child 6 $10/6; ☺9am-4pm) offers breathtaking views. For a casual walk or bike ride, the 8-mile **Recreation Path** wends its way along the Pemigewasset River and through the notch. Otherwise, the **Mt Pemigewasset Trail** begins at the Flume Visitor Center and climbs for 1.4 miles to the 2557ft summit of Mt Pemigewasset (Indian Head). It, too, has excellent views. Departing from **Lafayette Place campground** ( ☎603-823-9513; 97 sites; $16; ☺late May–mid-Oct), the **Lonesome Lake Trail** climbs 1000ft in 1½ miles.

## Beloved Poet

Robert Frost (1874-1963) spent some of the most inspired years of his life near Franconia. **The Frost Place** ( ☎603-823-5510; www.frostplace.org; Ridge Rd; adult/senior/child $3/2/1.25; 🕐 1-5pm Sat-Sun late May-Jun & 1-5pm Wed-Mon Jul–mid-Oct) is a memorial to his life and work. Many of his most famous poems describe life on this farm and the scenery surrounding it, including *The Road Not Taken* and *Stopping by Woods on a Snowy Evening*. Take I-93 north to Franconia, then NH 116 south. After a mile, turn right onto Bickford Hill Rd, and left onto unpaved Ridge Rd.

have unrestricted access. **Hancock Campground** ( 🕐year-round; 56 sites) is located near the East Branch of the omnipresent, refreshing Pemigewasset River. A hop, skip and a jump away, from the **Lincoln Woods Visitor Center**, head out on the 2.9-mile **Lincoln Woods Trail** (elevation 1157ft), among the easiest and most popular in the forest. Following an old railroad bed, the easy **Wilderness Trail** begins where the Lincoln Woods Trail ends, and it continues for 6 miles to Stillwater Junction (elevation 2060ft). It's popular with cross-country skiers and snowshoers. This area, known as the **Pemigewasset Wilderness Area**, is prime for backcountry hiking. From here the **Hancock Branch** of the Pemi River parallels the road and frames the mountains nicely. **Big Rock Campground** ( 🕐year-round; 28 sites) is the closest place for hiking in the **Greeley Ponds Scenic Area**.

As you start ascending the actual Kanc Pass, there are numerous scenic pullouts. As the road descends and starts to parallel the **Swift River**, don't miss lovely **Lily Pond**. Although you can't swim at **Sabbaday Falls Trail and Picnic Area**, take the rewarding 10-minute hike to the falls. Next up, the **Passaconaway Campground** ( 🕐mid-May–Oct; 33 sites) is on the eminently fishable Swift, just west of the **Passaconaway Historical Site**, a 19th-century house left over from the area's logging and farming days. If you can't do without hot showers and flush toilets, stop at **Jigger Johnson Campground** ( 🕐mid-May–mid-Oct; 75 sites). **Bear Notch Road** is a hard-packed gravel road that serves as a shortcut for those heading to Crawford Notch and US 302. Although there are some great viewpoints at the northern end, it's closed in winter, when it's well used by cross-country skiers. Just down the road, the 3-mile **Champney Falls Trail** provides relatively easy access to a nice waterfall. Nowhere along the route will you see more people than at the **Lower Falls Scenic Area**, a great place for picnicking alongside a popular swimming hole. Practically next door, the **Blackberry Crossing Campground** ( 🕐year-round; 26 sites) is a mere six miles west of Conway, as is **Covered Bridge Campground** ( 🕐mid-May–mid-Oct; 49 sites), the only campsite that accepts reservations, and one reached via the authentic **Albany Covered Bridge** (1858). Stop at the **Saco River Ranger Station** ( ☎603-447-5448; 🕐8am-4:30pm in winter, 8am-5:30pm Jul-Aug) west of Conway for any questions.

# NORTH CONWAY

## Population 2070

The Kanc's eastern terminus is Conway, but the region's activities capital is North Conway, 5 miles north. Auto traffic on Main St (NH 16 and US 302) often moves at a glacial pace. The **Mt Washington Valley Chamber of Commerce** ( ☎603-356-3171, 800-367-3364; www.mtwashingtonvalley.org; NH 16 and US 302) is south of the town center. The outfitter **EMS** ( ☎603-356-5433; Main St) sells maps to the WMNF and rents camping equipment, cross-country skis and snowshoes.

## SIGHTS & ACTIVITIES

### CONWAY SCENIC RAILROAD
☎603-356-5251, 800-232-5251; www.conwayscenic.com; coach/1st-class: adult $37/44, child $21/30; ⏰11am mid-Sep–mid-Oct; Tue-Thu & Sat mid-Jun–mid-Sep
Of the three trips offered here, the 'Notch Train' is New England's most stunning rail journey. It covers 50 miles in 5½ hours as it passes through Crawford Notch.

### ECHO LAKE STATE PARK
☎603-356-2672; River Rd; $3
Two miles west of North Conway via River Rd, this placid mountain lake (great for swimming and picnicking) lies at the foot of White Horse Ledge, a sheer rock wall. A scenic road leads up to the 700ft-high Cathedral Ledge with panoramic White Mountains views.

### ATTITASH BEAR PEAK SKI RESORT
☎603-374-2368, 877-677-7669 snow report, 800-223-7669 lodging; www.attitash.com; US 302
Attitash offers mountain-bike rentals and trail access as well as guided horseback riding trips from mid-June to mid-October. Off-season, chairlifts whisk you up to the **Alpine Slide**, a long track that you schuss down on a little cart. Oh yeah, you can ski too.

### SACO BOUND INC
☎603-447-2177; www.sacobound.com; US 302; ⏰ mid-Apr–mid-Oct
Two miles east of Center Conway, these folks rent canoes and kayaks ($25.50 daily) and organize guided Saco River trips ranging from a few hours to a few days.

## SLEEPING & EATING

### ALBERT B LESTER MEMORIAL HI-AYH HOSTEL
☎603-447-1001; www.conwayhostel.com; 36 Washington St, Conway; dorm from $20, r from $48
This 43-bed place off NH 16 also has excellent hiking and bicycling opportunities just outside the door. Canoeists can easily portage to two nearby rivers.

### CRANMORE INN

☎603-356-5502, 800-526-5502; www.cranmoreinn.com; 80 Kearsarge St; d from $109

Among North Conway's most reliable values for decades, the Cranmore has 18 rooms with traditional country decor.

### CABERNET INN

☎603-356-4704, 800-866-4704; www.cabernet inn.com; NH 16; d $79-$179

These 11 guest rooms, within a thoroughly renovated 1840 house, have antiques, queen beds and fireplaces or spas.

### SHALIMAR

☎603-356-0123; 27 Seavey St; lunch $5-7, dinner $9-13; ⏱11am-2:30pm Tue-Sun, 5-10pm

This friendly Indian restaurant has tasteful decor and tasty dishes.

### CAFE NOCHE

☎603-447-5050; NH 16, Conway; dishes $8-10

You'll find some of the best Mexican food north of the Massachusetts border at this festive cafe.

### HORSEFEATHERS

☎603-356-2687; Main St; dishes $7-19

The town's most popular gathering place has an encyclopedic menu of pasta, salads, sandwiches, burgers, bar snacks and main courses.

---

## DETOUR: MT WASHINGTON

The Northeast's tallest **mountain** (6288ft; www.mountwashington.com) is renowned for frighteningly bad weather. At times, it mimics Antarctica's; hurricane-force winds blow every three days or so, and the summit temps average a mere 26.5°F. Serious hikers should consult the **Appalachian Mountain Club** (AMC; ☎603-466-2727, 800-262-4455; www.amc-nh.org; Pinkham Notch Camp, US 302). You can ascend by car via the 8-mile **Mt Washington Auto Rd** ( ☎603-466-2222; www.mt-washington.com; $18 for car & driver; $4-7 per additional passenger; ⏱ early May-late Oct, weather permitting.) Take NH16 north from North Conway.

The quaintest way to reach Mt Washington is via the **Cog Railway** ( ☎603-278-5404, 800-922-8825; www.thecog.com; adult/senior/child $49/45/35; ⏱ 8:30am-4:30pm weekends early May-early Jun; 8:30am-4:30pm daily early Jun-late Oct). Since 1869, coal-fired steam-powered locomotives have followed a 3½-mile track up the second-steepest railway track in the world. Make reservations by phone. Reaching the cog railway is a joy: Take US 302 west for 32 miles from North Conway through dramatic Crawford Notch (1773ft), past the grand and imposing **Mount Washington Hotel** ( ☎603-278-1000; www.mtwashington.com; from $269, including meals).

# ROUTE 9

VT 9 links hip and funky Brattleboro, on the fertile Connecticut River Valley, with Bennington, bordering the Taconic Mountains of New York state. Along the way it slices through the Green Mountain National Forest, rich with summer hiking and winter snowshoeing and skiing possibilities.

While Vermont is one of the most rural states in the union, these two towns are among its most populous. But ironically, the stretch between them is one of the least. VT 9 is also called the Molly Stark Trail, named for the wife of General Stark, the hero of the Revolutionary War's Battle of Bennington. Along and off VT 9 you'll encounter covered bridges, good backcountry dirt roads, rivers, mountains and farms. It's a particularly lovely drive during fall foliage season, but it's also quite well traveled during that time. The state's name, by the way, is drawn from the French *vert mont*, which means 'green mountain.'

From Boston, take MA 2 west to Greenfield to I-91 north for Brattleboro (125 miles; 2½ hours). To return to Boston from Bennington, take US 7 south to Williamstown (Mass) to MA 2 east (165 miles; 3¼ hours).

# BRATTLEBORO

## Population 12,000

The site of Vermont's first colonial settlement (1724), Brattleboro is a pleasant, compact place with a groovy feel: This is where the USA's 1960s 'alternative' lifestyle settled down to live. You'll see lefty political literature, a few tattoo parlors and a lot of male facial hair. Bratt's sturdy red-brick buildings house some fine pubs, outdoor gear shops and artisanal galleries. The **Brattleboro Chamber of Commerce** ( ☎ 802-254-4565; www.brattleboro.com; 180 Main St) publishes a good map.

## SIGHTS & ACTIVITIES

### COVERED BRIDGES

Windham County has 30 of these architectural and historical beauties; stop at the chamber of commerce for a brochure pinpointing them. To reach Vermont's 'longest, still-used' bridge, head north on VT 30 to West Dummerston.

### BRATTLEBORO BICYCLE SHOP
☎ 802-254-8644; 178 Main St

Feel like tooling around more than 200 miles of backcountry dirt roads? Didn't bring those kinds of wheels? These folks rent hybrid bicycles ($20 daily) and are an excellent source of information about where to use them.

## VERMONT CANOE TOURING
☎ 802-257-5008; 451 Putney Rd

For rentals and guided canoe and kayak jaunts down the lazy Connecticut or West Rivers, these folks rule the waters. To find this outfitter, head north on US 5 (Putney Rd) to Veterans Memorial Bridge where the West and Connecticut rivers meet.

## ROBB FAMILY FARM
☎ 802-254-7664; 888-318-9087; www.robbfamilyfarm.com; 827 Ames Hill Rd;
🕑 10am-5pm Mon, Tue & Thu-Sat, 1-5pm Sun

Maple sugaring and Vermont are practically synonymous. You can witness the magical, sugary transformation at this 400-plus-acre family farm. In autumn, the Robb family also offers hayrides, and in winter sleigh rides (call ahead for reservations). Head west on VT 9, left on Green Leaf Rd, go through the stop sign and up Ames Hill Rd.

# SLEEPING & EATING

## FORT DUMMER STATE PARK
☎ 802-254-2610, 888-409-7579; www.vtstateparks.com; Old Guilford Rd; sites $14-23; 🕑 mid-May–early Sep

This 217-acre park has 51 sites, 10 lean-to shelters, hot showers and nature trails. Head north on US 5, then a half-mile east on Fairground Rd, then a mile south on Main St to Old Guilford Rd.

## LATCHIS HOTEL
☎ 802-254-6300; www.latchis.com; 50 Main St; r/ste from $65/145

Built in the 1930s by Demetrius Latchis, a Greek immigrant successful in the fruit business, the nicely restored art deco landmark has 30 comfortably renovated, but simple rooms. It's one of the area's more interesting places to stay. Hoist a pint of Olde Guilford Porter at the **Windham Brewery** ( ☎ 802-254-4747), downstairs.

## CROSBY HOUSE
☎ 802-257-4914, 800-528-1868; www.crosbyhouse.com; 45 Western Ave; d from $130

This perfectly restored mid-19th-century mansion has three guest rooms decorated with great care and comfort.

## BRATTLEBORO FOOD CO-OP
☎ 802-257-0236; Canal St; 🕑 8am-9pm

This excellent, earthy place is a purveyor of whole food groceries and organic produce. The incredible cheese department offers more than 500 distinct varieties, dozens of which are made on small Vermont farms. There isn't a better cheese selection in Vermont.

## AMY'S BAKERY ARTS CAFE
☎ 802-251-1071; 113 Main St; lunch $3-5; 🕑 8am-6pm Mon-Sat, 10am-5pm Sun

Enjoy your breakfast breads, pastries and coffee complete with close-up views of the river and local art. At lunchtime, the offerings revolve around salads, soups and sandwiches. You can't go wrong here.

## TJ BUCKLEY'S

☎ 802-257-4922, 132 Elliot St; mains $25-30; ⏲ 6- 9:30pm Thu-Sun

This upscale-but-classic, tiny and authentic 1927 diner seats just 18, but those lucky 18 are in for an exceptional dinner. The menu changes nightly, and locals rave that TJ Buckley's food is Brattleboro's best.

# ON THE ROAD

Heading west on VT 9 through **West Brattleboro**, past the reconstructed **Creamery Bridge** (1879), the flat valley opens up with broad views and winds along Whetstone Brook past tiny sugarhouses and farms selling maple syrup.

The first village you'll reach, **Marlboro** (population 985), appears pretty but unremarkable. The 1-mile detour into town takes you past old rock walls, stands of birches and cleared fields to a practically perfect white meeting house, a white inn, a white village office building and a few white houses. To chamber-music lovers, though, Marlboro looms large because of the **Marlboro Music Fest** ( ☎ 802-254-2394 after April 1; www.marlboromusic.org; tickets $5-30; ⏲ weekends Jul–mid-Aug), which is alive with enthusiastic music students and concertgoers. Reserve seats in advance.

Back on VT 9, take **Augur Hole Rd** 8 miles to **South Newfane**, just for the fun of it. This hard packed spur road leads past classic farms, alongside little Rock River and through the woods. Take the right split for South Newfane, through a **covered bridge** (1870) and past the **Williamsville General Store**. If you're still having fun, backtrack a few miles and take VT 30 north to **Newfane** (population 1700) proper. Arguably the most picturesque village in an area rife with them, Newfane boasts a handsome town green flanked with a Congregational church, stately courthouse and handsome inns. Backtrack to VT 9.

Continuing west on VT 9, **Hogback Mountain** (2410ft) provides a high vantage point for a marvelous '100-mile' view. The **Skyline Restaurant** ( ☎ 802-464-3536; dishes $7-10; hbreakfast & lunch Thu-Mon), complete with knotty pine decor, has homemade soups and traditional comfort foods. Just down the road, the 160-acre **Molly Stark State Park** ( ☎ 802-464-5460, 888-409-7579; www.vtstateparks.com; sites $14-23; hmid-May–mid-Oct) has 24 sites and 10 lean-tos and much appreciated hot showers. Take the **Mount Olga trail** to the top (2415ft), from which there are panoramic views.

**Wilmington** (population 2250) exists primarily to serve **Mt Snow/Haystack** ( ☎ 802-464-3333, 800-245-7669 lodging; www.mountsnow.com), one of New England's best ski resorts and an excellent summertime mountain-biking and golfing spot. You'll know you're close when traffic starts to bottleneck, eventually coughing up a collection of wooden buildings straight out of a Western. They've

## A Month in the Woods

America's first long-distance hiking trail, Vermont's **Long Trail** is an impressive 264-mile mountainous corridor that runs the length of the state. It crosses streams, skirts hidden ponds and wends along open ridges to bare summits. Wave after wave of hillside gently rolls back to a sea of green dotted with the occasional pasture or meadow. For more than a day trip, contact the **Green Mountain Club** (GMC; ☎802-244-7037; www.greenmountainclub.org).

been converted to country stores, clothing stores, artisan galleries and eateries.

As for area lodgings, the **Nutmeg Inn** (☎802-464-3351, 800-277-5402; www.nutmeginn.com, VT 9; d from $169) is a fine 18th-century renovated farmhouse with 14 rooms and suites furnished with antiques and reproductions. For cheap sustenance, quick service and excellent chili, **Dot's** (☎802-464-7284; VT 100; dishes $3-8.25; ☽ 5:30am-8pm) is popular. Skiers tend to scarf down steak and eggs for breakfast. Attractive and casual, the **Maple Leaf Malt & Brewing** (☎802-464-9900; 3 N Main St; dishes $6-17; ☽lunch & dinner) obliges with local microbrews, apps, a hearty steak, and live entertainment. It offers a good respite.

Back on the road, VT 9 climbs and eventually opens up onto the enormous Harriman reservoir, a nice place for a picnic.

Between blink-and-you'll-miss-it Searsburg at VT 8 and Bennington, there are numerous trailheads for hiking deep into the Green Mountain National Forest. The **Appalachian Trail** (aka **Long Tail** in Vermont) also crosses VT 9, offering a colorful hiking experience during fall foliage. As a base for exploring, camp at **Woodford State Park** (☎802-447-7169, 888-409-7579; www.vtstate parks.com; VT 9; sites $14-23; hmid-May–early Sep), with 82 sites and 20 lean-tos, a beach, boat and canoe rentals and hiking trails.

In **Woodford** (population 414), the **Prospect Mountain Cross-Country Ski Touring Center** (☎802-442-2575; www.prospectmountain.com) offers more than 40km of groomed trails, lessons and ski rentals.

# BENNINGTON

### Population 15,700

Bennington, a felicitous mix of picture-perfect Vermont (Old Bennington) and workaday town (Bennington proper), is also home to prestigious Bennington College. It's a historic place, famed for the crucial Battle of Bennington during the Revolutionary War. Three classic covered bridges are found just off VT 67A in North Bennington. Especially noteworthy is the silk-covered bridge (1899) on Silk Rd. The

**Bennington Area Chamber of Commerce** ( ☎802-447-3311, 800-299-0252; www.bennington.com; US 7) publishes a driving tour for bridges and a walking tour of Old Bennington. US 7 is known as North St and VT 9 as Main St. Do stop at **Bennington Museum** ( ☎802-447-1571; www.benningtonmuseum.com; W Main St; adult/seniors & students/child $8/7/ free; ⊙ 9am-5pm), which boasts a rich collection of paintings by Anna Mary Moses (1860–1961), a New York farm wife. At the age of 70, when she could no longer keep up with the heavy physical demands of farm labor, 'Grandma Moses' began to paint.

A mile west of downtown on W Main St, colonial **Old Bennington** is the prize for coming so far. It's nestled on an utterly charming hilltop site and studded with 80 substantial Georgian and Federal houses (dating from 1761 to 1830) arranged along a broad mall. The Palladian **Old First Church** is noted for its churchyard and draped fencing, which holds the remains of five Vermont governors, numerous Revolutionary War soldiers and poet Robert Frost. Views from the **Bennington Battle Monument** ( ☎802-447-0550; Monument Ave; adult/child $1.50/75¢; ⊙ 9am-5pm mid-Apr–Oct) are quite impressive. Don't miss riding to the top of the obelisk. Continue on VT 9A toward the New York border for 360-degree hilltop of the surrounding mountains.

## SLEEPING & EATING

### MOLLY STARK INN B&B
☎802-442-9631, 800-356-3076; www.mollystarkinn.com; 1067 Main St; r $70-105, cottage $135-160
A big 1890 Victorian with six comfy guest rooms, the inn also boasts a private honeymoon cottage and two sugar-house suites with vaulted ceilings, hardwood floors and a double-sided fireplace.

### SOUTH SHIRE INN
☎802-447-3839, www.southshire.com; 124 Elm St; d from $110
This antique-filled Victorian inn has nine rooms, some with fireplaces.

### ALLDAYS & ONIONS
☎802-447-0043; 519 Main St; breakfast & lunch $4-7, dinner $15-19;
⊙ 7:30am-3pm Mon-Sat, 5-9pm Tue-Sat
This popular storefront eatery prepares creative sandwiches, salads and soups by day. By night, try roasted turkey with mashed potatoes.

### RATTLESNAKE CAFÉ
☎802-447-7018; 230 North St; dinner $6-16
The local Mexican joint traffics in hefty bean-and-cheese burritos and strong margaritas.

# ROUTE 100

**MAP 9, VERMONT**                    **168 MILES; 3-5 DAYS**

Vermont is one of the most rural states in the union and the state's scenic highway slices right through its heart. VT 100 snakes north from the Massachusetts border, along the backbone of the Green Mountains, and almost to Quebec. The landscape consists of rolling farmlands as green as billiard felt and littered with cows, along backcountry roads where the only traffic is the local farmer's tractor. We're talking tiny villages with white Congregational churches and white, mid-19th-century clapboard homes converted into inns.

The heart of central Vermont, north of Killington, features some of New England's most bucolic countryside. This is where cows begin to outnumber people. Outdoors enthusiasts make frequent pilgrimages here to ski and mountain bike, while urban hipsters browse in antique shops and art galleries. Then there are the covered bridges.

Vermont is busiest in winter, when its slopes burst with skiers, snowboarders and tubers. But if you want to see lush green pastures, summer is more splendid, and fall foliage is positively glorious.

To reach the southern terminus from Boston, take MA 2 west to I-91 north to exit 2 in Brattleboro. From here take VT 9 west to VT 100 north (132 miles; 2½ hours). To return to Boston from Stowe, take I-89 south to I-93 south (205 miles; 3½ hours). After this completely scenic drive, fear not I-89 and I-91; they're among the country's most bucolic.

# ON THE ROAD

From **Wilmington** (see VT 9, p50), head north on VT 100. Tiny **West Dover**, lined with a handful of perfect white clapboard buildings, is the jumping off point for the **Mount Snow** ( ☎ 802-464-3333, 800-245-7669 lodging; www.mountsnow.com) ski area atop **Haystack Mountain**. In summer, Mt Snow offers lots of hiking possibilities and hosts one of the country's best mountain-biking schools. The slopes loom in the distance as you begin passing hillsides that have been shaved of trees, essential for farming and raising Jersey cows. Ski chalets dot the landscape as often as hay bales.

Climb and then descend (at a 10% grade) VT 100 into **West Wardsboro**, a blink-of-an-eye village laced with a disproportionate number of red wooden buildings. For the first of many fine side road detours, consider taking the **Arlington/Kelly Stand Road** west out of town. After about 6 miles, turnoff for Grout Pond and Somerset Reservoir, around which there are easy hiking trails.

Back on VT 100, **Wardsboro** (population 854) is more blue collar, its houses topped with corrugated tin roofs. Just beyond, **Jamaica** (population 946), on the other hand, appeals to an upscale crowd. Drive through in a heartbeat or settle in for a few days. Among the handful of buildings are a proud church, a few fine galleries, the ever-classic **Jamaica Country Market** (VT 100) and the **Three Mountain Inn** ( ☎ 802-874-4140, 800-532-9399; www .threemountaininn.com; VT 30/100; $145-325). Just up the road the 750-acre **Jamaica State Park** ( ☎ 802-874-4600, 888-409-7579; www.vtstateparks.com; sites $16-23; ☯ mid-Apr–mid-Oct) could easily reel you in with good hiking, swimming and camping at 61 sites and 18 lean-tos.

Make a quick detour south on VT 30 from **West Townshend** for the **Scott Covered Bridge,** Vermont's 'longest single span' bridge. Both West Townshend and Townshend provide worthy picture possibilities.

Pastures are divided by posts strung with barbed wire; hilltop farmsteads are delineated by a solitary farmhouse. Sagging barns, open vistas and rolling fields lead to **South Londonderry**, where the ultra gourmet **Village Pantry de Logis** ( ☎ 802-824-9800; VT 100; ☯ 7am-7pm Sun-Thu, 7am-10pm Fri-Sat) rewards patient drivers with roasted chicken, fine cheeses, crusty bread and specialty creations. Just north in **Londonderry** (population 1730), **Jake's Marketplace Cafe** ( ☎ 802-824-6614; jct VT 100 & 11; dishes from $7; ☯ weekends for lunch, nightly for dinner), a long-lived sports bar, serves mighty sandwiches and, at dinner, more substantial pizzas, steaks and pasta dishes.

Next up is **Weston** (population 620), an absolutely pristine village, its common ringed in wrought iron and graced with towering maples and a bandstand. Weston is perhaps most known as home to the **Vermont Country Store** ( ☎ 802-824-3184; VT 100; ☯ 9am-5pm Mon-Sat), which reigns supreme as purveyor of all that's unnecessary but all that makes life's little chores easier. The store is an experience in nostalgia, humor and Yankee ingenuity. You will undoubtedly leave with a handful of charmingly eccentric items that you'll use fondly for years. The **Weston Playhouse** ( ☎ 802-824-5288; www.westonplayhouse.org; tickets $22-45; ☯ late Jun–mid-Oct), Vermont's oldest professional theater, enjoys a fine reputation. Arrive early for a show or to dine on light fare 'Downstairs at the Playhouse.' For overnighting, the **Darling Family Inn** ( ☎ 802-824-3223; www.thedarlingfamilyinn.com; VT 100; d $85-145), an 1830s farmhouse with lovely antiques, has five rooms and two cottages; hospitality here is pure Vermont!

**Ludlow** (population 958) is dominated physically and psychologically by **Okemo** ( ☎ 802-228-4041, 800-786-5366 lodging; VT 100) and its ski area and state park. With more than 700 condos in its rental pool, Okemo has the area lodging covered. Rentals are cheaper in the summer than winter. In nearby **Proctorsville** (population 958), the **Golden Stage Inn** ( ☎ 802-226-7744, 800-253-8226; www.goldenstageinn.com; Depot St; d $79-300) offers one of the coziest overnight stays in the area. This former 18th-century stagecoach stop, off VT 103 east, is an 11-room inn with views of the mountain. Take a 5-mile detour west on VT 103 to **Healdville** and stop in to watch cheese being made at the **Crowley Cheese Factory** ( ☎ 802-259-2340; Healdville Rd; factory ☯ 8am-4pm weekdays, cheese shop ☯ 11am-5:30pm). They've been doing it since the 1820s.

Back on VT 100 a string of lakes provides a cool change of scenery from endless forest and farmland before reaching VT 100A for **Plymouth** (population 555). Calvin Coolidge (1872–1933) was born and sworn in here as the 30th US president when word reached him of Harding's sudden death in 1923. Calvin's father, the local justice of the peace, administered the presidential oath of office by kerosene lamp. Don't miss stopping at the tranquil and perfectly manicured **Coolidge Homestead** (☎802-672-3773; VT 100A; adult/children $6.50/ free; ☀ tours 9:30am-5pm late May–mid-Oct). Calvin is buried in the local cemetery. Also on the grounds, you can sample the goods at the **Plymouth Cheese Company**. A good Vermont cheese can melt in your mouth like butter or it can have the sharpness of a dry white wine. Best to start knowing the difference.

At the junction of US 4, take a 6-mile detour to sample the suds at the **Long Trail Brewing Company** (☎802-672-5011; US 4, Bridgewater Corners), where freshness is redefined.

# KILLINGTON MOUNTAIN
## Population 1100

Back on VT 100, as expansive mountain vistas unfold in layers before your eyes, you're confronted with Vermont's largest **ski resort** (☎802-422-3333, 800-621-6867; www.killington.com). Not a skier? Killington boasts top-notch facilities for every conceivable winter activity. Not a winter person? Whatever the season, it's all about outdoor activities here, and it's all centrally located on the mountain. The **Killington Chamber of Commerce** (☎802-773-4181; www.killingtonchamber.com; US 4/VT 100) provides details.

The **Mountain Bike & Repair Shop** (☎802-422-6232; Killington Rd) rents wheels ($50 daily). Ride the K-1 gondola to the Killington summit and whiz down 45 miles of trails. Bike trails cost $8 daily; gondola and trails are $30. As for hiking, the shop has an excellent (free) map of 14 self-guided trails. If you simply want to ride the **gondola**, it costs $9/5/20 adult/senior & child/family.

## SLEEPING & EATING
### GIFFORD WOODS STATE PARK
☎802-775-5354, 888-409-7579; www.vtstateparks.com; Gifford Woods Rd; sites $16-23; ☀ late May-early Oct
A half-mile north of US 4 and VT 100, this 114-acre park has 27 campsites, 21 lean-tos, a playground, hiking trails and fishing in Kent Pond.

### KILLINGTON LODGING SERVICE
☎800-621-6867; www.killington.com
The resort's central reservation agency is the best source for area lodging.

### CASEY'S CABOOSE
☎ 802-422-3795; Killington Rd; dishes $15-26

A great family eatery with salads and burgers available throughout the day, Casey's is also fun during happy hour.

### MOTHER SHAPIRO'S
☎ 802-422-9933; Killington Rd; dishes $3-10

By far the area's most popular place for breaking the morning fast, Mother's also serves juicy burgers and killer-size sandwiches. The service is as friendly as the portions are hefty.

### THE VERMONT INN
☎ 802-775-0708; US 4; dinner $18-22

Presided over by an award-winning chef who prepares a mean rack of lamb and steaks without slighting vegetarians, the inn offers one of the mountain's best dining values.

# ON THE ROAD

North of Killington, VT 100 is one of the finest stretches of road in the country – a bucolic mix of rolling hills and farmland so fertile you'll feel like jumping out of the car and digging your hands in the soil. As VT 100 widens and flirts with the White

## Ski Resorts

Families like the diverse terrain at **Mt Snow** ( ☎ 800-245-7669, 802-464-2151 snow reports; www.mountsnow.com), with 132 trails and 60 miles of cross-country routes.

**Okemo** ( ☎ 802-228-5222 snow reports; www.okemo.com), a big-time mountain with a small-time feel, boasts a 4.5-mile run.

With a season that runs from early November to late May, **Killington** ( ☎ 802-422-3333, 800-621-6867; www.killington.com) is prime. The mountain offers 200 runs on seven mountains, a vertical drop of more than 3000ft and great lifts.

Downhill skiing at **Sugarbush** ( ☎ 802-583-2381, 802-583-7669 snow report; www.sugarbush.com) means flying down serpentine trails, around corners and through tight slots, always in the company of trees.

**Mad River Glen** ( ☎ 802-496-3551; www.madriverglen.com) is the East's nastiest lift-served ski area, a combination of rocks, ice, trees – and snow, of course. Subaru wagons with Vermont license plates often have bumper stickers that dare, 'Mad River Glen, Ski It If You Can.'

**Stowe** ( ☎ 802-253-7311, 800-253-4754; www.stowe.com) is the best-regarded ski resort in the eastern USA; the variety of terrain is unparalleled. Let's say you're new to the sport, your partner's an expert and the kids love bopping down the intermediate slopes. No worries here.

River, darting to and fro across the valley floor, you'll encounter plenty of shimmering grain silos sheathed in aluminum caps. Weathered, peeling barnboard gives way to classic calendar views dotted with cows. Just for the fun of it, from **Talcville** take VT 73 across the mountain pass, or from **Hancock** (population 382), take VT 125. If you need a destination or excuse, let it be the lovely **Texas Falls**.

Between the two, pick up provisions in the modestly happenin' village of **Rochester** (population 1170) at **Kristina's Kitchen** (☎802-767-4258; VT 100; 8am-5pm Mon-Sat, 9am-3pm Sun), serving espresso and healthy sandwiches. Before leaving head east for a couple of miles on the high **Bethel Mountain Rd**, simply to turn around and come back down. The panoramas are well worth it. Just north on VT 100, pop into the **Green Mountain National Forest Visitor Center** (☎802-767-4261; 8am-4:30pm Mon-Fri year-round, 8am-4:30pm Sat in summer). Next stop, **Granville Gulf Reservation** (VT 100), a dark, winding and narrow 6-mile stretch with a state park, picnic area, falls and a charming roadside maple syrup purveyor.

Tiny, tiny **Warren** (population 1680) boasts the countrified **Warren Store** (☎802-496-3864; Main St), where you can enjoy a deli sandwich in a spot outside overlooking the waterfall. Across the street, the luxuriously comfortable **Pitcher Inn** (☎802-496-6350; 888-867-4824; www.pitcherinn.com; d from $330), with 11 artful rooms, has a dining room that's equally elegant, pricey and worthy. For a memorable side trip from Warren village, take Brook Rd to Roxbury Gap Rd and turn left onto **E Warren Rd**, which deposits you at a covered bridge in Waitsfield center.

# WAITSFIELD

## Population 1660

Perhaps you've seen Warren and Waitsfield in Vermont tourism ads. They're places where nothing ever changes. This is especially true for **Mad River Glen** (p56) and **Sugarbush** (p56), which feature New England skiing of yore, when trails were cut by hand and weren't much wider than hiking paths. Even though Waitsfield has a couple of tasteful strip malls, its heart consists of double-hung storefronts and a warren of galleries and shops near the 1833 **Village Bridge**. Since Vermont's soul resides along her spur roads, don't miss **Bragg Hill Rd** just north of the junction of VT 100 and VT 17. Stop at the **Sugarbush Chamber of Commerce** (☎802-496-3409, 800-828-4748; www.madrivervalley.com; VT 100).

Canoeing and kayaking are prime on the Mad and White rivers (along VT 100) from April to early June. **Clearwater Sports** (☎802-496-2708; VT 100) rents canoes ($30-50 daily), kayaks, river-floating tubes, inline skates, bicycles ($20 daily), snowshoes, telemark demo gear, and many other types of sports equipment.

## SLEEPING & EATING

### SUGARBUSH VILLAGE
☎ 800-451-4326; www.sugarbushvillage.com; $90-550
The folks here rent the area's largest selection of condos.

### INN AT MAD RIVER BARN
☎ 802-496-3310, 800-631-0466; www.madriverbarn.com; VT 17; d $95-110; ☽ Jul-Mar
One of the last old-time Vermont lodges, this place rents 15 rooms, some of which are in the annex with queen-size beds, steam baths and TVs.

### INN AT ROUND BARN FARM
☎ 802-496-2276, 800-721-8029; www.theroundbarn.com; 1661 E Warren Rd; d $130-295
This decidedly upscale inn features 12 guest rooms with gas fireplaces, canopy beds and antiques. Its name is derived from the adjacent 1910 round barn, one of the few remaining in Vermont. The barn's lower level has an indoor 60ft-lap pool; outdoor pursuits revolve around snowshoeing, cross-country skiing and off-road driving.

### AMERICAN FLATBREAD
☎ 802-496-8856; VT 100; flatbreads $9-18; ☽ dinner Fri-Sat
The excellent pizza pies made here are cooked in a primitive wood-fired oven. In fact, the Revolution Flatbread is so good that it's distributed to grocery stores throughout New England.

### SPOTTED COW
☎ 802-496-5151; Bridge St Marketplace; dinner $17-25; ☽ Tue-Sun
Just off VT 100, locals rave about the Bermudian fish chowder, but then again, the lunchtime smoked chicken salad and dinnertime pan-fried rainbow trout are excellent, too.

### JOHN EGAN'S BIG WORLD PUB AND GRILL
☎ 802-496-3033; VT 100; dinner $10-17
Don't let the exterior decor deter you. Extreme skier John Egan has hired a renowned chef from Montpelier's New England Culinary Institute. Venison and lamb dishes are arguably Vermont's finest.

# ON THE ROAD

A particularly brilliant stretch of VT 100 continues through the broad Mad River Valley: barns hug the roadside, silos stand as sentinels guarding disappearing family farms and Mount Mansfield (4393ft) looms in the distance. The old town of **Waterbury** (population 4925), wedged between a traffic light and some railroad tracks, isn't much to write home about, but this is where you'll return to catch I-89.

# STOWE

### Population 4340

In a cozy valley where the West Branch River flows into the Little River, Stowe has a certain commercial, Vermont-style charm. Its small center is pretty without being prim. The lodging and eateries lining Mountain Rd (VT 108) up to the ski slopes have adopted central European names to go with their architecture. By all means, continue up VT 108 through the rocky gorge known as Smugglers Notch, a true highlight for coming so far. (The notch is closed in winter.) The **Stowe Area Association** ( ☎ 802-253-7321, 800-247-8693; www.gostowe.com; Main St) is well organized.

## SIGHTS & ACTIVITIES

### COLD HOLLOW CIDER MILL
☎ 802-244-8771; VT 100

New England's largest producer of fresh apple cider also stocks other Vermont goodies like maple syrup and cheddar cheese.

### CROSS-COUNTRY SKIING

The **Trapp Family Lodge** ( ☎ 802-253-8511; www.trappfamily.com), famous because of matriarch Maria von Trapp, has made Stowe the Northeast's premier cross-country skiing destination. But the **Edson Hill Nordic Center** ( ☎ 802-253-8954) has much to offer, too, including $12 trail passes and $18 equipment rentals.

### HIKING

The **Stowe Recreation Path**, for bicycle, roller-skate and foot traffic only, follows the course of the Waterbury River (and Mountain Rd) for 5.3 miles. **The Green Mountain Club** ( ☎ 802-244-7037; www.greenmountainclub.org; 4711 Waterbury-Stowe Rd, Waterbury Center) publishes some excellent hikers' materials available from their office five miles south of Stowe.

### BICYCLING

Several bike shops can supply you with wheels for cruising along the Recreation Path, including **Mountain Sports & Bike Shop** ( ☎ 802-253-7919; 580 Mountain Rd; $11/25 per 2 hr/day for recreation path bikes, $20/30 per 4 hr/day for mountain bikes).

### SNOWSHOEING

**Tubbs Snowshoes** ( ☎ 802-253-7398) are manufactured in Stowe and you can purchase or rent them at **Umiak Outdoor Outfitters** (below). Umiak guides also lead popular three-hour snowshoeing jaunts, lit by headlamp or moonlight, for $39 per person.

### CANOEING & KAYAKING

**Umiak Outdoor Outfitters** ( ☎ 802-253-2317; www.umiak.com; 849 S Main St) rents canoes and kayaks ($32-42 daily) and offers two- and four-hour lake and river shuttle trips ($25-35 per person).

## Ben & Jerry

Years ago, childhood buddies Ben Cohen and Jerry Greenfield sent away $5 for information about how to make ice cream. They opened up shop in an unused gas station in Burlington, dispensing unorthodox flavor combinations. As super-premium ice cream became wildly popular, Ben and Jerry took their operation nationwide. Although they later sold out to the European conglomerate Unilever, Ben and Jerry remain on the board of directors and operate a charitable foundation funded by the sale of the company. Popular **factory tours** are offered ( ☎886-258-6877; VT 100; adult/senior $3/2; ⊙ 9am-8pm Jul-Aug, 10am-6pm Sep-May, 9am-5pm Jun).

# SLEEPING

### SMUGGLERS NOTCH STATE PARK
☎802-253-4014, 888-409-7579; www.vtstateparks.com; 7248 Mountain Rd; sites $16-23; ⊙late May–mid-Oct

This 25-acre park, 8 miles northwest of Stowe, has just 20 sites and 14 lean-tos.

### FIDDLER'S GREEN INN
☎802-253-8124, 800-882-5346; www.fiddlersgreeninn.com; 4859 Mountain Rd; d $65-125

An 1820s farmhouse with rustic pine walls, a fieldstone fireplace and seven guest rooms, Fiddler's Green is geared to outdoor enthusiasts. Guests congregate around the fieldstone hearth; it's all quite homey.

### BRASS LANTERN INN B&B
☎802-253-2229, 800-729-2980; www.brasslanterninn.com; VT 100; d $95-225

Just north of town, this beautifully renovated inn has nine spacious rooms with fireplaces, stenciling, antiques and quilts.

### TRAPP FAMILY LODGE
☎802-253-8511, 800-826-7000; www.trappfamily.com; 700 Trapp Hill Rd; d $198-379

Off Luce Hill Rd from Mountain Rd, the hills are alive with the sound of tourism at this Austrian-style chalet, built by the actual Maria von Trapp whose story inspired *The Sound of Music*. The 2700-acre spread has 116 motel and lodge rooms, as well as time-share units.

### TOPNOTCH AT STOWE
☎802-253-8585, 800-451-8686; www.topnotchresort.com; 4000 Mountain Rd; d $180-345

Stowe's most lavish resort has 92 rooms and really is top-notch. If your wallet can handle it, inquire about its townhouses. Amenities include a spa, bar, fine dining, outdoor pool, indoor and outdoor tennis courts, skating rink and touring center.

# EATING & ENTERTAINMENT

### HARVEST MARKET
☎ 802-253-3800; 1031 Mountain Rd; ⌚ 7am-7pm
This one-stop gourmet purveyor dishes out cold entrées by the pound, wonderful Vermont cheeses, crusty loaves of bread, salads and sandwiches.

### DUTCH PANCAKE CAFÉ
☎ 802-253-8921; 900 Mountain Rd; dishes $5.50-9.50; ⌚ 7:30am-12:30pm
Within the Grey Fox Inn, the Dutch owner makes more than 75 kinds of *pannekoeken* (Dutch pancakes). Some have a Southern twist, with sausage and gravy.

### MIGUEL'S STOWE AWAY
☎ 802-253-7574; 3148 Mountain Rd; dishes $9-16; ⌚ noon-3pm & 5-10pm
This Mexican farmhouse cantina became so popular that it launched its own nationally-distributed line of chips and salsa. You'll find Tex-Mex, gringo and creative dishes like salmon with a mango-poblano sauce.

### GRACIE'S RESTAURANT
☎ 802-253-8741; Main St; lunch $5-15, dinner $8-23
Gracie's, following Miguel's, is becoming so popular that supermarkets around the country now carry Gracie's sauces. Specialties include big burgers, hand-cut steaks, Waldorf salad and garlic-laden shrimp scampi.

### BLUE MOON CAFE
☎ 802-253-7006; 35 School St; dinner $16.50-26
In a converted house with a little sunporch, this intimate bistro is among New England's top restaurants. Entrées change nightly, but they're usually sublime. Look for Maine crabs, salmon dishes, oysters, rabbit and an extensive wine list.

### MATTERHORN
☎ 802-253-8198; 4969 Mountain Rd; cover $5; bands Fri-Sat
At the top of Mountain Rd, this place is always hopping by 5pm, when skiers start to hobble off the slopes.

### CHARLIE B'S
☎ 802-253-7355; 1746 Mountain Rd
If you're searching for an après-ski scene with a bit more class, Charlie B's at the Stoweflake Inn has it.

### THE SHED
☎ 802-253-4364; 1859 Mountain Rd; ⌚ 11:30am-10pm
This cozy microbrewery always has six fresh beers on tap.

# INDEX